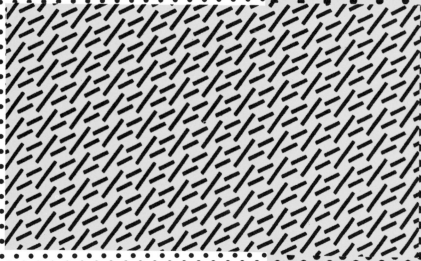

THE NEW

FROM CALIFORNIA

LOGO

THE NEW LOGO

FROM CALIFORNIA

DESIGNED & EDITED BY
GERRY ROSENTSWIEG

PUBLISHED BY
MADISON SQUARE PRESS

While Madison Square Press makes every effort possible
to publish full and correct credits for each work included in
this volume, sometimes errors of omission or commission
may occur. For this we are most regretful, but hereby must
disclaim any liability.

This book is printed in four-color process, a few of the
designs reproduced here may appear to be slightly different
than in their original reproduction.

ISBN 0-942604-28-8
Library of Congress Catalog Card Number 92-0614 49

Distributors to the trade in the United States and Canada:
Van Nostrand Reinhold 115 Fifth Avenue, NY 10003

Distributed throughout the rest of the world by:
Hearst Books International 1350 Avenue of the Americas
New York, NY 10019

Publisher:
Madison Square Press 10 East 23rd Street, New York, NY 10010

Editor: Gerry Rosentswieg
Designer: The Graphics Studio

PRINTED IN HONG KONG

CONTENTS

5

AnonymousGraphics
European, 1930-1935
Logo for, a steelworks.

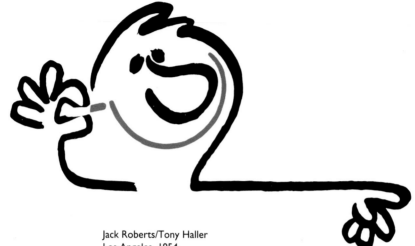

Jack Roberts/Tony Haller
Los Angeles, 1954
AD: Jack Roberts
Illus: Tony Haller
Logo designed to illustrate
the Carson Roberts
advertising agency slogan,
"Have a happy day"

Ken Parkhurst
Los Angeles, 1954
Ken Parkhurst & Associates
Logo for Playhouse Pictures,
a film production firm.

Anonymous Graphics
European, 1930-1935
Logo for hat manufacturer.

INTRODUCTION

Back in the days when few people could read, pictures substituted
for words. Although it may be fading fast, literacy is relatively new.
In the good old days, tradespeople put a sign over their shop picturing
what they were selling. These signs were the first brandmarks --
the first logos. For years, simple signs depicting bread, beer, anvils,
harnesses and other commodities were commonplace, informational
symbols. In some places, such signs still hang over shops. Now they're
considered picturesque.

It was only a matter of time until symbols began appearing on labels
and packaging, helping to identify brand names for those who could
read and many who could not. From there it wasn't a very large step
to using symbols to identify the companies who made the products
and other businesses, as well. Symbols were shortcuts. They were
easy to recognize and often carried a message, sometimes subtle,
sometimes not, about the product or company they represented.

Early marks were pretty straightforward, but as competition became a
factor, humor, puns, satire and even whimsey began slipping into the
pictures. Reddy Kilowatt, the electric company symbol, may have been
dumped in the name of progress, but Mr. Peanut is still around, still carry-
ing his cane and still looking at us through his monacle. Both were
designed to identify a product and used a light touch to tell us about it.

Every period of art is a reaction to the period that precedes it. It is no
different in graphic design. The styles in the late nineteenth and early
twentieth centuries were, for the most part, personal statements. The
posters and advertising in Paris during the Belle Epoque, the style and

grace of the materials created in England during the Edwardian era and the Viennese Secessionist movement were all hands-on movements. After the First World War, Art Deco was the style that captured the European imagination with a cross between the mechanical shapes of the draftsman and the artist's irrepressible spirits.

In the years just before World War II, some remarkable marks began to appear. They were strong, clever, highly imaginative and subjective. They look as good today as they did then. In fact, you might have a problem judging which mark was created in 1934 and which was hot off the drawing board. Perhaps that should be hot out of the computer! But somewhere between the personal statements made in the '20s and '30s and the corporate agenda of the '80s, the trademark grew increasingly refined and distilled.

As mainstream corporations grew larger and more diversified, the logos created for them became more abstract, until the mark and the company had little to do with each other. Many of the best and most widely used marks were difficult to identify--abstractions that don't reveal anything about the company they represent.

Anonymous Graphics
European, 1930-1935
Logo for automotive spplies.

But recently, humor and whimsy and the touch of the artist's hand began to slip back into the picture. That's what stimulated this book; it is what I call the "new" logo. The marks are more quirky; what's new is beginning to look a lot like what's old. The charm and personality of the past has a decidedly '90 s look and flavor. More eclectic, more colorful and more subjective.

The "new" logo is not necessarily a new phenomenon. There have always been those marks, usually created for small, creative companies that relied upon personality, wit and charm. Often the marks were created for designers and agencies for self promotion. But today, led by the music and entertainment industries, and followed closely by the clothing and computer industries, the "new" logo is appearing more often. This is particularly true where the market is young and casual, and the logos can make a statement about whom they represent. The "new" logo is here, certainly in small companies and in many programs for larger corporations, as well. Their influence is growing. The Fortune 500 better watch out!

Gerry Rosentswieg
11. 15. 92

Anonymous Graphics
European, 1930-1935
Logo for hair
care products.

10.1

11.1

11.2

11.3

HAIR CUTS

TABOO

12.1

GUESS   WHERE?

PARTY

12.2

12.1
Clive Piercy
Los Angeles, 1988
Ph.D
AD: Clive Piercy/Michael Hodgson
Logo for a hair salon. The 'X'
shape is meant to be the ultimate
taboo symbol.

12.2
Clive Piercy
Los Angeles, 1990
Ph.D
AD: Clive Piercy/Michael Hodgson
Symbol exploited for use as a
party invitation.

13.1
Jay Vigon
Los Angeles, 1987
Client: Leon Max
Logo for a women's clothing
company showing the designer
juggling with influences, trends
and the market.

13.2
Susan Rogers
Santa Monica, 1992
Rusty Kay & Associates
AD: Rusty Kay
Logo for a toy store showing
a child at play and the joy of
being a kid.

13.1

13.2

14.1
Mark Fox
San Rafael, 1990
Black Dog
AD: Lauren Watson
Ag: Foote, Cone & Belding
Client: Levi Strauss
Logo for The Big Jean, a looser
fitting jean for boys. The phrase above
the figure is an anagram for
"The Big Jean".

14.2
Michael Vanderbyl
San Francisco, 1990
Vanderbyl Design
Logo designed for an appearance
at The Western Art Directors Club.

15.1
Susan Rogers
Santa Monica, 1990
Rusty Kay Associates
AD: Rusty Kay
Logo for a garage showing "the
power of the wrench, the might
of the mechanic".

15.2
Steven M. Isaksons
San Francisco, 1992
Logo for Bodymaster,
sportswear store.

15.3
Mitchell Mauk
San Francisco, 1991
Mauk Design
Logo for MacWeek Magazine's Target
Award. The mark signifies a company
with a product that has hit the target.
15.4
The logo with type application.

15.5
Neal Zimmermann/Tim Clark
San Francisco, 1990
Zimmermann Crowe Design
AD: Neal Zimmermann/Dennis Crowe
Illustrator: Tim Clark
Logo for Hero Presentation Printing,
a short-run printer.

14.1

14.2

RUSTY'S
OCEAN PARK MOTORS

15.1

15.3

15.4

15.2

15.5

ELECTRONIC ARTS CELEBRATES IT'S TEN YEAR ANNIVERSARY OF CREATIVELY PLAYING AROUND

10 E|A

16.1

16.1
Ruediger Goetz
San Francisco, 1992
Zimmermann Crowe Design
AD: Dennis Crowe
Logo for Electronic Arts, a computer
games manufacturer.

17.1
Gerry Rosentswieg
Los Angeles, 1992
The Graphics Studio
Logo for The Amie Karen Cancer
Fund/LA Marathon fundraising
promotion. The mark signifies the fun
of being involved in the run.

17.2
Michael Patrick Cronan
San Francisco, 1990
Cronan Design
Logo for Walking Man,
a clothing collection.
17.3
Shown with Walking Man icons.

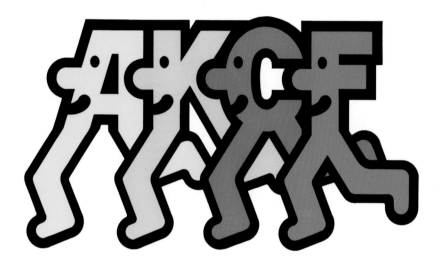

17.1

17. 2

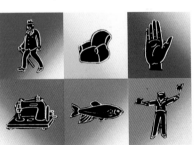

17.3

18.1

18.3

18.2

18.4

18.1
James McKiernan
Long Beach, 1991
McKiernan Studio
Logo for Organizational Support
Services, a company that plans
meetings and travel services. It is
intended to mean speed and creativity.

18.2
Paul Woods
San Francisco, 1991
Woods + Woods
Logo for Apple Computer/Adobe
Systems to imply competition and
cooperation as in the Olympics.

18.3
Dennis Crowe
San Francisco, 1988
Zimmermann Crowe Design
This logo was created when the
company was formed to show the
energy of a design partnership.

18.4
Romane Cameron
Los Angeles, 1991
Studio Seireeni
AD: Richard Seireeni
Logo for a retail store that specializes
in athletic shoes.

19.1
Jay Vigon
Los Angeles, 1986
Vigon Seireeni
Man-fish logo for a men's surfwear
manufacturer.

19.2
Paul Woods
San Francisco, 1992
Woods + Woods
A visual pun of a spotlighted
"dandy" for a candy company.

19

19.1

19.2

20.1

20.3

20.2

20.4

20.1
Stan Evenson
Los Angeles, 1991
Stan Evenson Design
Logo for BrooksHoward, Inc.,
a company that duplicates video, CD
and cassettes.

20.2
Earl Gee/Fani Chung
San Francisco, 1991
Earl Gee Design
Logo for the San Francisco Arts
Commission program of performance
and visual art enhancing the use and
enjoyment of public transit on Market
Street.

20.3
Raymond Wood
Los Angeles, 1992
Bright & Associates
AD: Keith Bright
Logo indicating fast delivery of
Chinese food.

20.4
Sarajo Frieden
Los Angeles, 1990
Sarajo Frieden Studio
Icon developed for use in
a book store.

21.1
Mark Fox
San Rafael, 1990
Black Dog
AD: Mary Ann Dibs
Client: Warner Bros Records
Symbol for a two-man band, *Unity 2*.
Unity is expressed as singlemindedness,
literally.

21.2
Jay Vigon
Los Angeles, 1988
Vigon Seireeni
AD: Sheri Mobley
Logo for The Fashion Group. The
mark indicates the admission of men to
a previously restricted organization and
was used as the theme of their annual
benefit.

21.3
Romane Cameron
Los Angeles, 1990
Studio Seireeni
AD: Richard Seireeni
Logo for a film production company,
South Schwartz, depicting the
combined creative energies of the two
women principals.

21.1

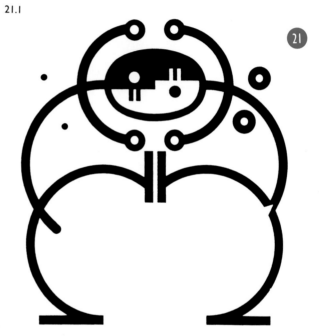

21.2

21.3

22.1

22.2

22.3

22.1
Bob Aufuldish
Larkspur, 1990
Aufuldish & Warinner
Self-promotional logo used on
whimsical, ephemeral items.

22.2
Larry Vigon/Brian Jackson
Los Angeles, 1991
Larry Vigon Studio
AD: Larry Vigon
Double "P" logo for Paris Photo.

22.3
Mark Fox
San Rafael, 1990
Black Dog
Logo for a photographer, showing the
camera's eye as a disembodied element.

23.1
Scott Mires
San Diego, 1990
Mires Design
Studio Logo, the designer personified.

23.2
Mark Fox
San Rafael, 1990
Black Dog
Logo for a small printing firm. The letter
"T" shows the printer with a stack of paper.

23.3
John Sabel
Los Angeles, 1990
Rod Dyer Group
AD: Rod Dyer
The logo indicates a robotic form associated
with the term digital and is intended to look
progressive and modern.

23.4
Vic Zauderer
San Francisco, 1992
Clement Mok Designs
AD: Clement Mok
Logo for Padcom, a pharmaceuticals testing
company, indicating the company's use
of penbased software to compile data.

23.5
Ross Hogan
Los Angeles, 1991
Ross Hogan Designs
Logo for a photographer indicating the ability
to shoot anything and anyplace in the world,
as well as a pun on the photographers name.

23.1

23.2

DIGITAL MUSIC EXPRESS

23.3

23.4

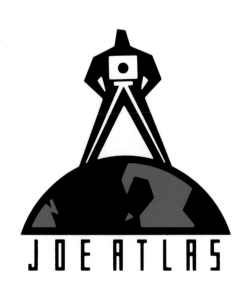

JOE ATLAS

23.5

24.1

24.2

24.1
Mark Fox
San Rafael, 1992
Black Dog
Logo monogram for William Mosgrove
"He's either shooting a picture or his head is
exploding, depending on your stress level".

24.2
Larry Vigon/Brian Jackson
Los Angeles, 1991
Larry Vigon Studio
AD: Larry Vigon
Logo for a division of a movie
production company.

24.3
Mike Salisbury
Los Angeles, 1990
Mike Salisbury Communications
AD: Mike Salisbury
Illustrator: Mark Kawagami
Logo for Michael Mann Productions, a TV
and film production company.

25.1
Michael Manwaring
San Francisco, 1985
The Office of Michael Manwaring
Logo/creature composed of diverse
parts for Heffalump, a toy store.
It is intended to imply an imaginative,
non-mass culture approach to
children's toys.

25.2
Anonymous Graphics
Los Angeles, 1988
Logo/icon designed for a
Los Angeles Magazine article
on the "Best Handymen".

24.3

25.1

25.2

26.1
Mark Fox
San Rafael, 1992
Black Dog
AD: Aubyn Gwinn
Ag: Foote, Cone & Belding
Logo for a Levi's contest. The sweepstakes winner gets to go to the NBA All Star Game and be an honorary ball-boy.

26.2
Hank Fischer
Venice, 1992
Fischer Design
Self-promotional logo.

27.1
Margo Chase
Los Angeles, 1991
Margo Chase Design
Logo for an Ocean Pacific skateboard promotion.

27.2
Pamela Racs
Los Angeles, 1991
Mark Taper Forum Graphics.
Logo for a theatrical piece about the Mexican revolution from a child's perspective. It is intended to convey a feeling of Mexican roots and heritage.

26.1

26.2

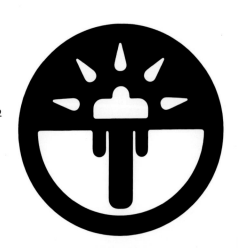

27.1

27.2

28.1

28.3

28.2

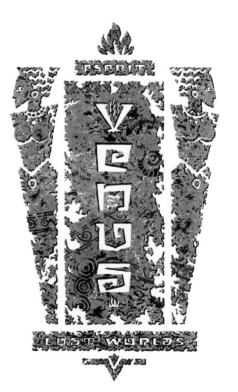

28.4

28

28.1
Jay Vigon
Los Angeles, 1989
Vigon Seireeni
AD: Jay Vigon/Richard Seireeni
Personal logo for Susie Stegmuler.

28.2
Jay Vigon
Los Angeles, 1991
Vigon Seireeni
AD: Jay Vigon/Richard Seireeni
Client: Flaming Collossus
Logo to publicize Sunday brunches
at a nightclub. This mark is called
Eat N' Joy.

28.3
Mark Fox
San Rafael, 1988
Black Dog
AD: Paul Huber
Ag: Altman & Manley
This logo symbolizes a joint venture
partnership between Apple Computer
and independent software developers.
The ad's idea was to represent
cooperative partnership by depicting
two one-winged creatures. In order
to fly they must be united.

28.4
Margo Chase
Los Angeles, 1987
Margo Chase Design
Client: Esprit
Logo intended to illustrate the theme
"Alien Artifacts" or archeology of the
future. It is a futuristic fossil that refers
both to the goddess and the planet
Venus.

29.1
Jay Vigon
Los Angeles, 1988
Vigon Seireeni
AD: Jay Vigon/Richard Seireeni
Logo for the Tamara Bane Gallery, the
sculptural female shape is intended to be
representative of the "out there" works
shown at the gallery.

29.1

30.1

30.3

30.2

PROJECT
ANGEL
FOOD

30.4

30.1
Anonymous Graphics
Los Angeles, 1987
Logo for a women's clothing shop.

30.2
Anthony D'Agostino
Los Angeles, 1987
Logo for the Los Angeles Center for
the Living, an AIDS support organization,
indicating a joy for life and a caring
interactive environment.

30.3
Peter Sellars/Rod Dyer
Los Angeles, 1989
Rod Dyer Group
AD: Rod Dyer
Logo for the Los Angeles Festival. It is
intended to show the diversity of the
entertainment offered and the cultural
diversity of the Los Angeles audience.

30.4
Anthony D'Agostino
Los Angeles, 1988
Logo for a service which brings hot
meals to AIDS patients unable to shop
and cook for themselves.

31.1
Brad Maur
Sacramento, 1991
Page Design
AD: Paul Page
Logo for a highly technical scanning
device that emphasizes the human and
compassionate qualities of the patients
for whom it is intended.

31.2
Landor Associates
San Francisco, 1991
Logo for American Conservatory
Theatre depicting an actor on
stage.

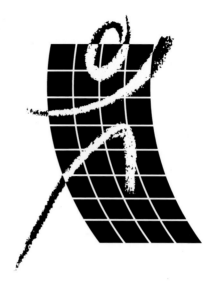

31.1

31.2

32.1

32.2

32.3

32.1
Earl Gee
San Francisco, 1991
Earl Gee Design
Fit @ Sun is the Sun Microsystems
employee fitness center. The logo
is intended to symbolize mental
and physical well-being.

32.2
Stan Evenson
Los Angeles, 1992
Stan Evenson Design
Logo for The American Child
Foundation.

32.3
Landor Associates
San Francisco, 1992
Logo for an environmental
organization.

33.1
Wes Aoki
San Francisco, 1991
Aoki Design
Logo for Orches, a dance organiza-
tion; it is intended to express
non-traditional forms of dance.

33.2
Bennett Peji
San Diego, 1991
Bennett Peji Design
Logo for a hospital's work
rehabilitation program; it is meant
to show normal activity after
treatment or surgery.

33.3
Christine Haberstock
Los Angeles, 1990
Logo for a photographer's rep.
The "x" on the portfolio refers to
the company's name - Xtra.

33.4
Anonymous Graphics
Los Angeles, 1992
Logo for a catering company.

33.2

33.1

33.3

33.4

34.2

34.1

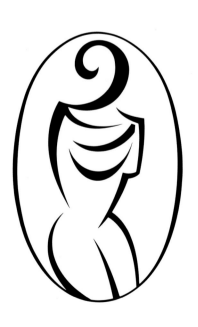

34.3

34.1
Christine Haberstock
Los Angeles, 1991
A logo for a woman's theatre. The
logo is intended to signify a woman
who is proud of her body and per-
sona and wants to be watched.

34.2
Steve Tolleson
San Francisco, 1992
Tolleson Design
Logo for a building.

34.3
Jay Vigon
Los Angeles, 1992
Jay Vigon Studio
Logo for a women's fashion
manufacturer. The logo is meant to show
a hangar draped with a woman's form.

35.1
Romane Cameron
Los Angeles, 1992
Studio Seireeni
AD: Richard Seireeni
The logo is meant to indicate a fun place
to eat and listen to music.

35.2
Lorna Stovall
Los Angeles, 1989
Margo Chase Design
AD: Margo Chase
A logo created for a holiday promotion.

35.3
Lorna Stovall
Los Angeles, 1990
Lorna Stovall Design
The logo is intended to portray some of the
production services managed by the agency.

35.1

35.2

35.3

36.1

36.3

36.2

36.4

36.1
Romane Cameron
Los Angeles, 1990
Studio Seireeni
AD: Richard Seireeni
A mermaid is used to suggest
women's swimwear.

36.2
Arne Ratermanis/Ted Hansen
San Diego, 1989
Ted Hansen Design Associates
AD: Ted Hansen
This logo for Classic Reprographics, a
photo and blueprint reproduction house, is
meant to convey speed and dependability.
Casual research showed that the word
"classic" was associated most often with
cars, which prompted an old-fashioned
hood ornament look.

36.3
Gary Hannigan
Los Angeles, 1990
Hannigan & Schmidt
This logo for a messenger service is meant
to imply speed. It also refers to the logo of
the parent company Andresen Typographics.

36.4
Lucia Matioli
San Francisco, 1992
Mauk Design
AD: Mitchell Mauk
The client, a specialty silkscreener, came
with a favorite quote. "The arrow that finds
its mark begins as an idea in the mind of
the archer." The logo was based on this
quote and is intended to imply precision
and craftsmanship.

37.1
Larry Vigon/Brian Jackson
Los Angeles, 1990
Larry Vigon Studio
AD: Larry Vigon
Logo for a tailoring shop is meant
to convey style.

37.2
Steve Curry
Los Angeles, 1988
Curry Design
Logo is intended to be playful and
innovative; it indicates swimwear
for a younger market.

AMERICAN
T A I L O R I N G

37.1

TAKE COVER

37.2

38.1

38.2

THE MECHANICAL ARTIST

39.1

38.1
Anonymous Graphics
Los Angeles, 1985
Logo for a bar.

38.2
Mark Fox
San Rafael, 1988
Black Dog
AD: Michael Vanderbyl
Promotional logo for Esprit de Corp.

39.1
James Smith
Newport Beach, 1987
The Mechanical Artist
Promotional logo.

39.2
Michael Patrick Cronan
San Francisco, 1989
Cronan Design
Logo for Apple Industrial Group.

39.3
Michelle Svoboda
Laguna Beach, 1992
Red Top Design
Logo created for real estate
sales seminars.

39.2

39.3

40.1

40.1
Roberto Barazzuo
San Francisco, 1989
Studio Esprit
Promotional logo for clothing
manufacturer.

40.2
Sarajo Frieden
Los Angeles, 1990
Logo for a vintage clothing store.
The mark is intended to convey
style and attitude.

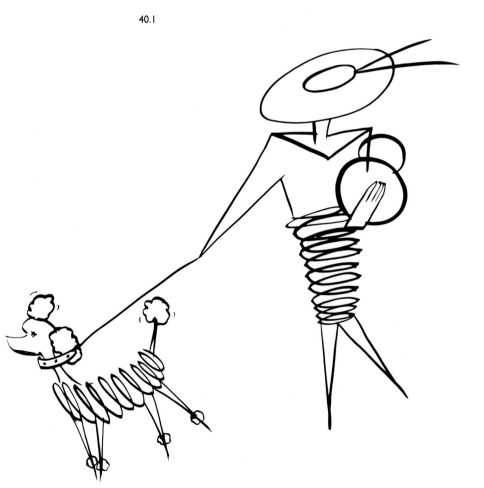

40.2

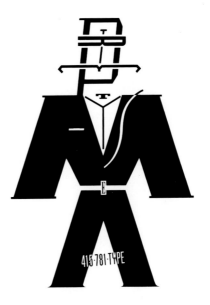

41.1

MASTERTYPE

ALPHAEXTENSIONS

41.2

41.1
Neal Zimmermann
San Francisco, 1991
Zimmermann/Crowe Design
AD: Neal Zimmermann/Dennis Crowe
Logogram made up of letterforms
spelling out MasterType.

41.2
Petrula Vrontikis/Bob Dinetz
Los Angeles, 1990
Vrontikis Design Office
AD: Petrula Vrontikis
This logo incorporates basic
principles used in Yoga-balance,
strength and flexibility. The form
is an important Yoga posture.

41.3
Mark Sackett
San Francisco, 1990
Sackett Design
AD: Mark Sackett
Illus: Mary Shea Duffek
The logo, for The Child Care
Employee Project, signifies
day care workers and the
children for whom they care.

41.3

42.1

42.2

42.3

42.1
Michael Vanderbyl
San Francisco, 1990
Vanderbyl Design
Logo for a Hawaiian, upscale,
resort community that overlooks
the commercial flower growing
region of Oahu.

42.2
Steve Curry
Los Angeles, 1992
Curry Design
Logo for a wine investment fund.
It is intended to show stability,
partnership and distinction.

42.3
John Pappas
San Francisco, 1990
Zimmermann Crowe Design
AD: Dennis Crowe
The logo, for an artists' rep, shows
two heads in profile, bisected by a
central figure. The head at left is the
client; the head on the right is the
artist. The central figure, the rep, is
the link between the two.

43.1
Raymond Wood
Los Angeles, 1989
Bright & Associates
AD: Keith Bright
A logo for Global Cleanup.

43.2 + 43.3
Romane Cameron
Los Angeles, 1992
Studio Seireeni
AD: Richard Seireeni
Illus: Tim Clark
Logos for various parts of
a large sports bar complex.

43.1

END ZONE

43.2

THE FAST BALL

SELF SERVICE TAKE OUT

43.3

43

44.1

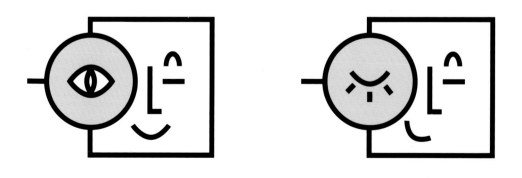

44.2   44.3

44.1
Mark Palmer
Palm Desert, 1988
Mark Palmer Design
Logo created for a national conference on depression. The stylized face looks depressed and is created with arrows to symbolize "New Directions in the Treatment of Depression".

44.2 + 44.3
Susan Rogers
Santa Monica, 1991
Rusty Kay & Associates
AD: Rusty Kay
Self-Promotional logos to suggest taking a closer look at the work of a studio that doesn't take itself too seriously.

45.1
Thomas McNulty
San Francisco, 1991
Profile Design
This cafe is located in the building where the Macintosh II was developed. The mark is based on the smiling face that comes on screen when one starts up. Apple calls him Megaman - the cafe is called Mega-Bite.

45.2
Steve Twigger
Los Angeles, 1988
Rod Dyer Group
AD: Rod Dyer
The logo for Mind Extension University, an education cable channel, that is meant to imply extending and enriching the mind.

45.3
Mark Fox
San Rafael, 1989
Black Dog
This logo, proposed for Rolling Pin Donuts, is meant to depict "someone sizing up a donut and simultaneously sizing up the viewer with a donut for a left eye. The client hated it."

45.1

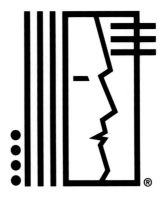

45.2

45.3

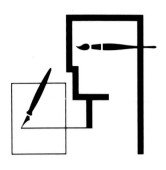

46.1

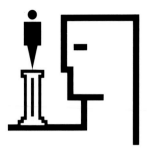

46.2

46.3

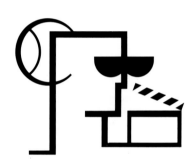

46.4

46.5

46.6

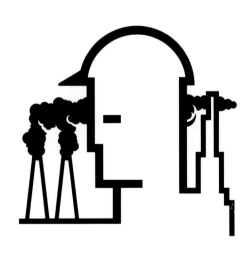

46.7

46.1 - 46.7
Jay Vigon
Los Angeles, 1987
AD: Rip Georges
These icons were designed to
accompany the annual Esquire
Magazine article that lists
people who deserve recognition in
various fields. The fields
are 46.1 Arts and Letters, 46.2
Sports and Style, 46.3 Philosophy,
46.4 Education and Social Services,
46.5 Politics and Law, 46.6
Science and Technology, 46.7
Business and Industry.

47.1
Larry Vigon/Brian Jackson
Los Angeles, 1990
Larry Vigon Studio
AD: Larry Vigon
Logo for Ocean Pacific's surfwear.

47.2
John Pappas
San Francisco, 1992
Zimmermann Crowe Design
AD: Dennis Crowe
Logo created for a line of sweatshirts
marketed as streetwear. The mark
suggests you don't have to workout
to wear these clothes.

47.3
Eve Morris
San Diego, 1992
Carol Kerr Graphic Design
Logo for a therapist. The mark suggests
the patients and families whose lives
have been fractured.

47.1

no sweat.

47.2

47.3

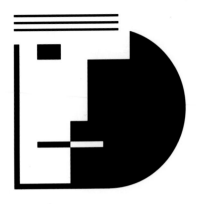

48.1

48.3

48.2

PIX

48.4

48.5

48

48.1
Dan McNulty
Los Angeles, 1991
McNulty & Co.
Logo for the Dobal Company,
a firm that handles talent
and produces movies.

48.2
Alfredo Muccino
Palo Alto, 1989
AD: Rick Tharp
Icon created for The Western Art
Directors Club magazine, for an article
"How to Have Your Way With Your
Clients".

48.3
James McKiernan
Long Beach, 1991
McKiernan Studio
Microphone logo for software company
meant to imply the human element in
computing.

48.4
Larry Vigon/Brian Jackson
Los Angeles, 1992
Larry Vigon Studio
AD: Larry Vigon
Logo for a photo supply house.

48.5
Jay Vigon
Los Angeles, 1989
AD: Mashisa Nakamura
Ag: Dentsu
Secondary logo/icon for a Japanese
radio station.

49.1
Mitchell Meeks
Los Angeles, 1991
Logo for opticians.

49.2
Larry Vigon/Brian Jackson
Los Angeles, 1992
Larry Vigon Studio
AD: Larry Vigon
Logo for a computer imaging firm.

49.1

49.2

50.1

50.1
Mike Salisbury/Terry Lamb
Los Angeles, 1988
Mike Salisbury Communications
AD: Mike Salisbury
Illus: Terry Lamb/Bob Zoell
Logo for clothing applications.

51.1
Ruediger Goetz
San Francisco, 1992
Zimmermann Crowe Design
AD: Neal Zimmermann/Dennis Crowe
Self-promotional logo for studio. It
playfully includes initials of the firm.

51.2
John Van Hamersveld
Los Angeles, 1970
Logo created for record albums and used
on a series of posters.

51.3
Larry Vigon/Brian Jackson
Los Angeles, 1992
Larry Vigon Studio
AD: Larry Vigon
Personal logo for a writer/actor.

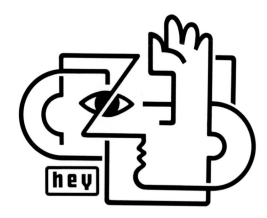

51.1

51.2

51.3

52.1

52.4

SKULD

52.2

52.5

52.3

52.1
Mark Fox
San Rafael, 1988
Black Dog
Logo for Mercury House,
a book publisher.

52.2
Jim Pezzullo
Los Angeles, 1990
Studio Seireeni
AD: Richard Seireeni
Skuld was one of the witches in Macbeth.
She was the one with the power to see
the future. Skuld is a corporate identity
consulting firm. The logo implies it is for-
ward thinking with an eye for design.

52.3
Mike Salisbury
Los Angeles, 1980
Mike Salisbury Communications
AD: Mike Salisbury
Illus: Robert Grossman
Self-promotional logo for the studio.

52.4
Michael Ward
Long Beach, 1991
McKiernan Studio
AD: James McKiernan
Logo for motorcycle accessories that is
meant to imply speed and adventure.

52.5
Arne Ratermanis
San Diego, 1990
Ted Hansen Design Associates
AD: Ted Hansen
Logo for an ocean front condominium
project that is intended to appeal to a
youthful market.

53.1
Rick Tharp
Los Gatos, 1991
Tharp Did It
Logo for The Dandy Candy Man,
purveyor of condiments.

53.2
Mark Fox
San Rafael, 1992
Black Dog
Logo for promotional
materials for Act Up!

53.1

COVER YOUR HEAD

WEAR A CONDOM!

53.2

54.1

54.1
Michael Patrick Cronan
San Francisco, 1992
Cronan Design
Icons for California College of
Arts and Crafts publication. The center
column of faces are CCAC.

55.1
Michael Cronan
San Francisco, 1992
Cronan Design
Logo created for above publication.

55.2
Ruediger Goetz
San Francisco, 1992
Zimmermann Crowe Design
Logo is a visual pun on the name Zipp,
as well as the idea that hairstyles are
temporary and can be changed often.

55.3
Ruediger Goetz
San Francisco, 1992
Zimmermann Crowe Design
AD: Dennis Crowe
Logo for a line of sweatsuits
"with attitude."

55.1

55.2

55.3

56.1

56.2

56.1
Lorna Stovall
Los Angeles, 1989
Margo Chase Design
AD: Margo Chase
Logo/Icon for hair care products and
meant to signify modern beauty.

56.2
Paul Curtin
San Francisco, 1990
Paul Curtin Design
Logo for Motto, a company
representing manufacturers of
contemporary furniture.

57.1
Pamela Racs
Los Angeles, 1991
Mark Taper Forum Graphics
Logo for a program of works in
progress; it is meant to convey a
rough unfinished quality.

57.2
Clive Piercy/Michael Hodgson
Santa Monica, 1990
Ph.D
Illus: Ann Field
The logo, for Aromatherapy
Seminars, is intended to evoke the
nature of aromatherapy.

57.3
Kathy Warinner
Larkspur, 1992
Aufuldish & Warinner
Logo for Tropo Music suggests
an interest in the music of other
cultures, as well as the "T" for
the company name.

57.4
Clive Piercy
Santa Monica, 1988
Ph.D
AD: Clive Piercy/Michael Hodgson
Illus: Anh Field
Logo for a studio of hair, make-up
and styling artists.

57.1

57.3

57

A R O M A T H E R A P Y

S E M I N A R S

57.2

57.4

58.1

58.1
Margo Chase
Los Angeles, 1987
Margo Chase Design
AD: Jeff Ayeroff
The "V" shaped man symbolizes the
cool attitude of the company's new
American division.

58.2
Melanie Doherty
San Francisco, 1990
Melanie Doherty Design
Illus: Anthony Russo
Logo for the Resort
at Squaw Creek.

59.1 + 59.2
Margo Chase
Los Angeles, 1988
Margo Chase Design
Logo for Esprit woman, a romantic
line, made up of figures and hearts.

59.3
John Pappas
San Francisco, 1990
Zimmermann Crowe Design
AD: Dennis Crowe
Logo for a heavy metal dance club,
Club 4808.

59.4
Bob Aufuldish
Larkspur, 1992
Aufuldish & Warinner
Logo for an industrial design educators'
conference. The theme of IDSA's conference was "making sense," which the client
defined as "making implies innovation,
while sense refers to the meaning
derived..." The head/spiral suggests the
focus involved in the design process, the
product of which is an idea, contained here
in a thought balloon, "making sense."

58.2

59.1

59.2

59.3

59.4

L I N D S T R O M

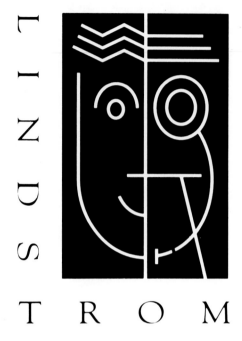

60.1

Innervision

60.2

60.1
Lauren Smith
Palo Alto, 1992
Logo for a photographer.

60.2
Rick Jackson
Irvine, 1991
Logo for a video production company
that specializes in self-help holistic tapes.

61.1
Maureen Erbe
Los Angeles, 1989
Logo for the Los Angeles Music Center's
Friday Noon Concert series, "Thank God
It's Friday."

61.2
Brian Collentine
San Francisco, 1985
AXO design studio
Logo for a community art center.

61.3
Margo Chase
Los Angeles, 1990
Margo Chase Design
Logo for a film production company.

61.4
Henry Rosenthal
Los Angeles, 1989
Rod Dyer Group
Logo for a television
production company suggesting
a sense of humor.

61.1

61.2

61.3

61.4

62.1

62.1
Philip Kim/Gary Davis
San Jose 1992
The Stephenz Group
AD: Rick Tharp/Stephanie Paulson
Logo designed to promote a social
program of the Western Art Directors
Club.

63.1
Kevin Mason
Los Angeles, 1991
Logo designed for a
leadership conference

63.2
Mark Fox
San Rafael, 1988
Black Dog
Poster icon for the San Francisco Art
Directors Club student portfolio review.
"a stare-off between two Bauhaus kinda
guys. The review is an event where
design professionals scan student portfo-
lios and offer advice, and students scan
professional and take notes on fashion
and designspeak."

63.3
Jay Vigon
Los Angeles, 1990
Vigon Seireeni
AD: Rip Georges
Editorial icon for an article entitled
'Vive le Difference" about the ethnic and
social diversity of the workplace.

63.4
Jay Vigon
Los Angeles, 1989
Logo for a sportswear company
called P.O.V., cameraman's term for
point of view.

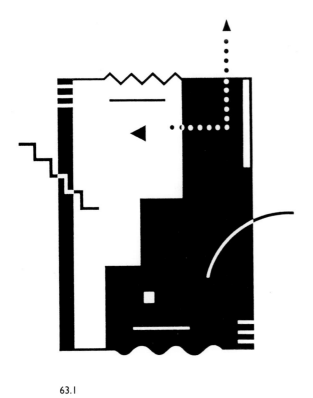

63.1

63.3

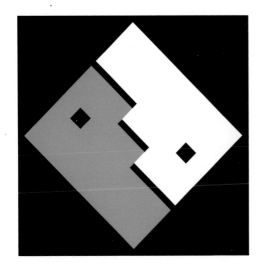

63.2

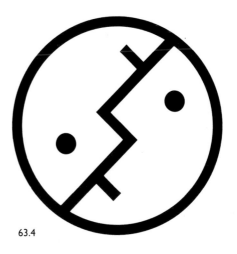

63.4

SHARKFIN™

64.1

64.1
Jay Vigon
Los Angeles, 1991
Logo for a wetsuit designed
for bodysurfing.

64.2
Jay Vigon
Los Angeles, 1992
Logo for a film production company.

65.1
Jay Vigon
Los Angeles, 1990
Vigon Seireeni
AD: Richard Seireeni
Logo for a restaurant/cabaret
featuring North African cuisine.
The image is based on the sort of
character one might have encountered
in Casablanca in the 1930's.

65.2
David Tillinghast
Los Angeles, 1991
Self-promotional mark
for an illustrator.

65.3
John L. Ball
Fresno, 1990
Solutions by Design
Logo for Language Enterprises,
multilingual interpreters.

FAHRENHEIT
FILMS

64.2

65.1

65.2

65.3

66.1

66.1
Paul Woods
San Francisco, 1992
Woods + Woods
Logo for a charity promotion
at a computer company.

66.2
Dan Magnussen
Palo Alto, 1987
Ag: Winston Advertising
Logo for Inner Beauty Dieticians

66.3
Bob Aufuldish
Larkspur, 1991
Aufuldish & Warinner
Personal logo.

67.1
Jay Vigon
Los Angeles, 1987
Vigon Seireeni
Rejected logo for a record project;
the mark was adopted as a promo
for the studio.

67.2
Jay Vigon
Los Angeles, 1992
Logo for a food product -- a
cone-shaped taco shell.

66.2

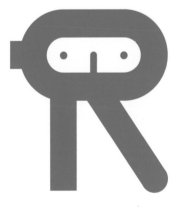

66.3

67.1

67.2

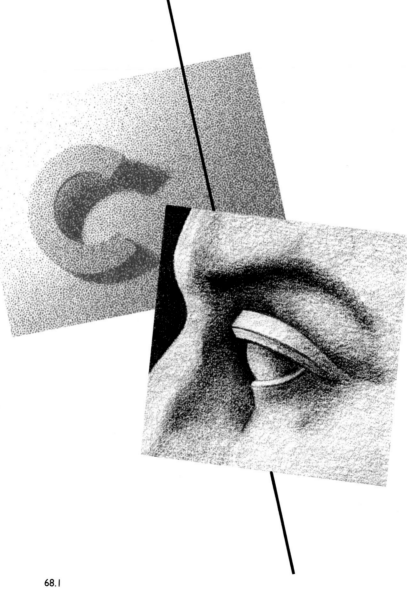

68.1

EYES
68.1
Steve Curry
Venice, 1991
Curry Design
Logo for the studio.

69.1
Paul Curtin
San Francisco, 1990
Paul Curtin Design
Studio Logo.

69.2
Mark Fox
San Rafael, 1990
Black Dog
Logo for a photographers' rep,
an eye with a flash.

69.3
Margo Chase/Lorna Stovall
Los Angeles, 1987
Margo Chase Design
AD: Margo Chase
Logo for a pop album cover that is
intended to look mystical and hip.

69

69.1

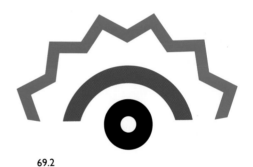

69.2

69.3

70.1

70.3

70.2

70.4

70.1
Margo Chase
Los Angeles, 1992
Margo Chase Design
Logo for a cable TV interview program.
The eye centered between the four
points of a compass represents a close
look at different personalities and
points of view.

70.2
Margo Chase
Los Angeles, 1989
Proposed logo for an advertising
agency. The eye refers to the visual
communication produce by the agency.

70.3
Margo Chase
Los Angeles, 1990
Margo Chase Design
Logo for Sidney Cooper. It is an
abstraction of the photographers'
eye, representing both the lens
and his personal vision.

70.4
Ruediger Goetz
San Francisco, 1992
Zimmermann Crowe Design
AD: Neal Zimmermann/Dennis Crowe
Promotional logo for the studio.

71.1
Thomas McNulty/Brian Jacobson
San Francisco, 1991
Profile Design
AD: Thomas McNulty
The Logo for Linda Graf, printing rep,
signifies her eye for detail when press-
checking printing.

71.2
Clive Piercy
Los Angeles, 1991
Ph.D
AD: Clive Piercy/Michael Hodgson
Logo for a record company. The
horizon type forms its own horizon
line through the eye. The symbol is
designed to evoke both primitive and
sophisticated associations.

71.3
Margo Chase
Los Angeles, 1989
Margo Chase Design
Logo for agency with the initials CCA.

71.1

71.2

71.3

72.1

72.2

72.1
John Van Hamersveld
Los Angeles, 1978
Logo for a publishing company,
New Visions/Lippincott.

72.2
Margo Chase
Los Angeles, 1991
Margo Chase Design
Logo for music video producer and
distributor.

73.1
Raymond Wood/Il Chung
Los Angeles, 1988
Bright & Associates
AD: Keith Bright
Logo for eyeglass stores. The eyebrow
swash shows fast service; the pupil
with 5 minute slice symbolizes speed,
indicating that you can get new glasses
while you wait.

73.2
Steve Tolleson
San Francisco, 1992
Anniversary logo for a computer
company.

73.3
Jay Vigon
Los Angeles, 1988
Logo for an art gallery specializing
in Russian avant garde art.

73.1

73.2

73.3

74.1

74.2

74.1
Margo Chase
Los Angeles, 1986
Margo Chase Design
Logo for a pop band. Lolita Pop is
slang for "peep show" in Sweden. The
mark incorporates eyes and lips. It is
intended to look hip, enigmatic and wild.

74.2
Jay Vigon
Los Angeles, 1990
Promotional logo for an artists' rep.

75.1
Wes Aoki
San Francisco, 1991
Aoki Design
Logo for image consultants. It is
intended to show the importance
of visuals in new products or
presentations.

75.2
William Reuter
San Francisco, 1990
William Reuter Design
Logo for Datavision Technologies
Corporation. The mark represents a
"D", an eye, and an ear to suggest the
interactive multimedia that the company
designs and develops.

75.3
John White/Maxine Mueller
Long Beach, 1991
White Design
AD: John White
Logo for a group of eye care
physicians with their practice is in the
area known as "the triangle".

75.4
Jay Vigon
Los Angeles, 1990
Self-promotional logo.

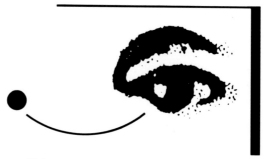

75.1

75.2

75.3

75.4

76.1

76.2

HANDS

76.1
Christine Haberstock
Los Angeles, 1992
Personal logo for illustrator/designer.
The fingers indicate creativity; the
cocoon signifies the constant meta-
morphosis of creativity.

76.2
Jay Vigon
Los Angeles, 1992
The logo indicates a hands-on approach
to a children's museum.

77.1
Howard Schneider
Rosemead, 1990
Personal Identity Logo.

77.2
Anonymous Graphics
Los Angeles, 1989
Logo for a speakers' bureau.

77.3
Paul Page/Linda Higgins
Sacramento, 1991
Page Design
AD: Paul Page
Logo for Institute for Local
Self Government.

77.1

77.2

77.3

78.1

78.2

78.1
Larry Vigon/Brian Jackson
Los Angeles, 1991
Larry Vigon Studio
AD: Larry Vigon
Logo for the studio.

78.2
Michael Manwaring
San Francisco, 1990
The Office of Michael Manwaring
Logo indicating that, despite
technology, good printing is the result
of craft.

79.1
Michael Manwaring
San Francisco, 1987
The Office of Michael Manwaring
Logo for a counseling center. The leaves
and hands suggest a humane and holistic
approach to counseling.

79.2
Anonymous
San Francisco, 1953
Logo for local bar called The Glad Hand.

79.3
Mark Fox
San Rafael, 1991
Black Dog
AD: Lisa Waltuch
Ag: The Mark Anderson Group
The logo represents a powerful software
program for professional programmers.

79.4
Melanie Doherty/Joan Folkmann
San Francisco, 1992
Melanie Doherty Design
AD: Melanie Doherty
Logo for a private high school with a
curriculum emphasizing fine and plastic
arts, as well as academics.

79.1

79.3

79.2

79.4

80.1

80.2

ANIMALS

80.1
Margo Chase
Los Angeles, 1992
Margo Chase Design
The logo for Dream Quest Images
symbolizes the ability that special effects
have to make fantasies real.

80.2
Kim Sage
Los Angeles, 1991
Vrontikis Design Office
AD: Petrula Vrontikis
The Pet Set is a fund raising arm of the
LASPCA. A generic animal, intended to
be smart, sassy and upbeat, and to
appeal to a young professional group.

81.1
Lindsay Loch
Los Angeles, 1990
Loch Design
AD: Liz Blackman
Logo for a gallery that shows
outsider art.

81.2
Anonymous Graphics
Los Angeles, 1991
Logo for a coffee house.

81.3
Larry Vigon/Brian Jackson
Los Angeles, 1989
Larry Vigon Studio
AD: Larry Vigon
Logo for Zuma Films

81.1

LIZARDS

81.2

81.3

82.1

82

82.4

82.2

82.5

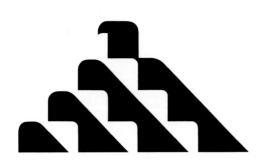

82.3

82.6

82.1
Mark Fox
San Rafael, 1990
Black Dog
AD: Andy Dreyfus
Logo for an in-house security system
for Apple. The logo is suggested by the
myth of ever-watchful Argus, the giant
with a hundred eyes.

82.2
Michael Manwaring
San Francisco, 1986
The Office of Michael Manwaring
Logo for a small, open air
shopping center.

82.3
Denis Parkhurst
Los Angeles, 1987
Ken Parkhurst & Associates
AD: Ken Parkhurst
Logo for an Arizona resort community
called Eagle Mountain.

82.4
Mark Fox
San Rafael, 1989
Black Dog
AD: Neal Zimmermann
Ag: Zimmermann Crowe Design
Promotional update of an existing
eagle logo.

82.5
Melanie Doherty
San Francisco, 1991
Melanie Doherty Design
Logo for an Italian restaurant; Gira
Polli means spinning chickens.

82.6
Bill Murphy
Los Angeles, 1988
Rod Dyer Group
AD: Rod Dyer
Logo for a fast food chain is
meant to imply that eating will be
fun and enjoyable.

83.1
Mamoru Shimokochi
Los Angeles, 1991
Shimokochi Reeves Design
Logo for a sporting goods company.

83.2
Margo Chase
Los Angeles, 1989
Margo Chase Design
Proposed logo for an organization
called "Save The Rainforest Monkey"

83.3
Anonymous Graphics
Los Angeles, 1992
Promotional logo.

83.1

83.2

83.3

84.1

84

84.2

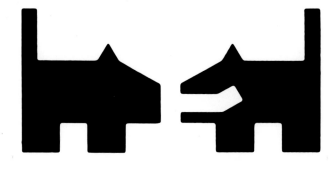

84.3

84.1
Mark Fox
San Rafael, 1989
Black Dog'
The logo is a rebus of the name
"Em-bark-O," for a restaurant
located on the embarcadero in
San Francisco.

84.2
Tony Hyun
Los Angeles, 1990
The Graphics Studio
AD: Gerry Rosentswieg
Proposed logo for LASPCA.

84.3
Patti Britton
Mill Valley, 1992
Logo for a retoucher.

85.1
Paul Curtin
San Francisco, 1991
Logo for a marketing consultant.

85.2
Jay Vigon
Los Angeles, 1990
Logo for a film production company.

85.3
Wayne Sakamoto
Mill Valley, 1992
Logo for a dog groomer.

85.4
Alan Disparte/Margo Chase
Los Angeles, 1992
Margo Chase Design
AD: Margo Chase
Logo for a Macintosh service bureau;
the whimsical dog reference is in the
style of its' namesake.

85.5
Mark Fox
San Rafael, 1985
Black Dog
"I used to have this sleazy job doing sleazy
paste-up for a sleazy advertising agency, and
whenever it got slow I'd create fake logos
for fake businesses. Black Dog was one of
them. It was only later that I realized this
snarling, fire-treading canine was something
of an alter ego, and as I was starting a fake
business myself, it seemed appropriate to
use the beast.

85.1

85.4

85.2

85.5

85.3

86.1

86.2

86.1
Mamoru Shimokochi
Los Angeles, 1990
Shimokochi Reeves Design
Logo for the Good Shepherd
Dental Laboratory.

86.2
Michael Schwab
Sausalito, 1987
Michael Schwab Design
AD: Michael Toth
Logo for a sweater company specializing
in natural wool products.

87.1
Jay Vigon
Los Angeles, 1989
Vigon Seireeni
AD: Kim Champagne
Logo for a band.

87.2
Mike Salisbury
Los Angeles, 1992
Mike Salisbury Communications
Secondary logo for a clothing company.
It is intended to mean that "cool cats"
wear this brand.

87.3
Steve Curry/Jason Scheideman
Los Angeles, 1991
Curry Design
AD: Steve Curry
Promotional logo for typographer's
Halloween material.

87.1

87.2

87.3

88.1

THE BLUE FOX

88.2

88.3

88.1
Gerald Reis/Albert Treskin
San Francisco, 1989
Gerald Reis & Company
Logo for a restaurant with a name taken from the "red light" district in Danville, CA, where it is located. The logo is designed to suggest neon-lit, back alley imagery.

88.2
Melanie Doherty/Christina Donna
San Francisco, 1988
Melanie Doherty Design
Restaurant logo.

88.3
Ward Schumaker
San Francisco, 1992
Restaurant Logo.

89.1
Stephen Black/Jonathan Meeks
San Rafael, 1992
Stephen Black Design
Logo for an art gallery.

89.2
Mike Salisbury/Terry Lamb
Los Angeles, 1991
Mike Salisbury Communications
AD: Mike Salisbury
Logo for Mattel games, indicating challenging, but fun games that are not too difficult.

89.3
Gunnar Swanson
Venice, 1988
Gunnar Swanson Design Office
Visual pun for a company that sells window coverings.

89.4
Michael Manwaring
San Francisco, 1978
The Office of Michael Manwaring
Logo for a specialty food store uses an ambiguous animal to represent the wide array of merchandise available.

89.5
Clement Mok
San Francisco, 1988
Clement Mok Designs
Studio logo indicating the California bear and the Macintosh Apple.

89.1

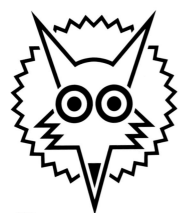

89.2

89.3

89.4

89.5

90.1

90.2

90.1
Glenn Martinez
Santa Rosa, 1990
Glenn Martinez and Associates
Logo for a tropical fish retailer.

90.2
Jay Vigon/Richard Seireeni
Los Angeles, 1987
Vigon Seireeni
Logo for a water-oriented
amusement park.

91.1
Mark Allen
Venice, 1991
Mark Allen Design Associates
Logo for a Mexican seafood restaurant.

91.2
Mark Fox
San Rafael, 1991
Black Dog
Logo for a seafood restaurant.

91.1

91.2

92.1

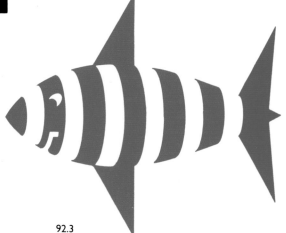

92.3

92.2

Fat Fish Films

92.4

T O N G A

93.1

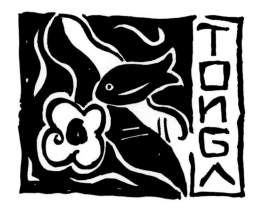

93.2

93.3

92.1
Jeanette Schraeder/Shelly Weir
San Francisco, 1989
Yashi Okita Design
AD: Yashi Okita
Logo for a seafood restaurant.

92.2
Margo Chase
Los Angeles, 1990
Margo Chase Design
Logo for a surfboard company.

92.3
Jay Vigon
Los Angeles, 1987
Vigon Seireeni
Proposed logo for
Wild Blue water park.

92.4
Jay Vigon
Los Angeles, 1992
Logo for a film production company.

93.1 - 93.3
Steve Curry/Jason Scheideman
Los Angeles, 1989
Curry Design
AD: Steve Curry
Promotional logos for a swimwear
and sportswear manufacturing
company. The logos take a playful
attitude to surf and beach objects.

EARTH ELEMENTS
94.1
Steve Curry
Los Angeles, 1988
Curry Design
Logo for a museum in Texas; the eclectic style reflects the various artifacts in the museum.

95.1
Scott Brown
Palo Alto, 1989
Michael Patrick Partners
AD: Dan O'Brien
Logo for a line of entertainment software for teen agers. The mark is intended to suggest that this is a fun and lively software company.

95.2
Anonymous Graphics
Palo Alto, 1990
Logo for a printing firm.

95.3
Mark Allen
Venice, 1990
Mark Allen Design Associates
Logo for a real estate development.

94.1

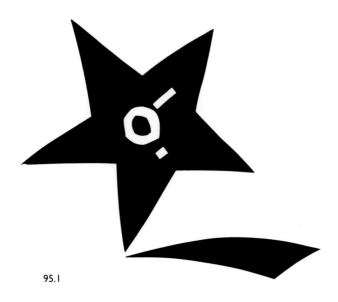

95.1

95.2

95.3

96.1

96.2

96.1
Clive Piercy
Santa Monica, 1988
Ph.D
AD: Clive Piercy/Michael Hodgson
Logo for a make-up, hair stylist and
photography representative. The mark
is intended to show a hip, progressive
and creative firm.

96.2
Patrick Soo Hoo/Katherine Lam
Los Angeles , 1989
Patrick Soo Hoo Designers
Logo that conveys a sense of
sun and fun.

97.1
Michael Manwaring
San Francisco, 1982
The Office of Michael Manwaring
Logo for winter sports condominiums.
It depicts snow and mountains within
a sun shape and is intended to portray
the beauty of winter.

97.2
Maureen Erbe
Los Angeles, 1992
Logo for a rideshare program,
intended to suggest that ridesharing
will clean the air and the world
we live in.

97.3
Sarajo Frieden
Los Angeles, 1990
Logo for Realworld Records,
intended to imply peacefulness,
harmony and humor.

97.4
Mark Fox
San Rafael, 1991
Black Dog
AD: Tom O'Grady
Logo for a professional
basketball team.

97.5
Sandra Koenig
San Francisco, 1991
Clement Mok Designs
AD: Sandra Koenig
Logo for a company that sells
interior accessories.

97.1

LOS ANGELES

COUNTY

RIDESHARE

97.2

97.3

97.4

PLACES IN

THE SUN

97.5

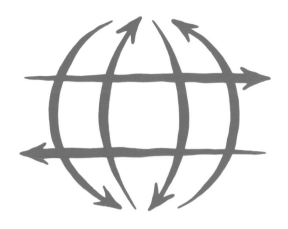

WORLDWIDE OPERATIONS

98.1

98.2

EARTH

98.3

98.1
Earl Gee/Fani Chung
San Francisco, 1991
Earl Gee Design
Logo and icons for worldwide opera-
tions of Sun Microsystems. The marks
embody the chairman's belief in "putting
all the weight behind one arrow."

98.2
Chuck Routhier
San Francisco, 1990
Clement Mok Designs
AD: Clement Mok
Logo for a worldwide conference.

98.3
Joseph Cortese
Carmel, 1992
Earth Art
Self-promotional logo.

99.1
Brooklyn 7
Los Angeles, 1990
Logo for an art park on the grounds
of a Frank Lloyd Wright residence.

99.2
Margo Chase
Los Angeles, 1991
Margo Chase Design
AD: Jessica Cusick
Logo for the art program for the
LA subway.

99.3
Ross Carron
San Francisco, 1989
Ross Carron Design
Illus: Carrole Jeung
Logo for a women's sportwear line.

99.1

99.2

99.3

100.1

100.2

100.3

100.1
Ruediger Goetz
San Francisco, 1992
Zimmermann Crowe Design
AD: Dennis Crowe
Logo to reinforce the idea of
world distribution.

100.2
Jeanne Kim/Kimberly Hillman
Venice, 1991
Warren Group
AD: Linda Warren
Illus: Joe Crabtree
Logo for a junior high school program
on the education of transportation.

100.3
Sally Hartman Morrow
San Francisco, 1991
Coleman Souter
AD: Mark Souter
Logo for a laptop fax system that
can go anywhere.

101.1
Romane Cameron
Los Angeles, 1992
Studio Seireeni
AD: Richard Seireeni
Illus: Tim Clark
Logo for a video arcade within a
sports bar complex; it is meant to
indicate electronic energy.

101.2
Rick Tharp/Jean Mogannam
Los Gatos, 1991
Tharp Did It
AD: Rick Tharp
Logo for software. The power of this
software is exemplified by the singular
cloud generating a bolt of lightning.

101.3 - 101.6
Romane Cameron
Los Angeles. 1991
Studio Seireeni
Series of logos that work together for
a high energy rap musician. Young M.C.
is the artist and the rest are song titles.

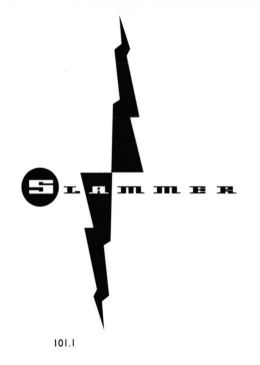

101.1

101.2

101.3

101.5

101.4

101.6

102.1

102.2

GROWING THINGS

102.1
Lorna Stovall
Los Angeles, 1990
Lorna Stovall Design
Personal logo that incorporates
an eye and a tryfuss, the three-legged
life force symbol that also signifies the
will to create.

102.2
Michael Brock
Los Angeles, 1989
Logo for Tumbleweed, a restaurant
featuring southwestern cuisine.

103.1
Michael Manwaring
San Francisco, 1981
The Office of Michael Manwaring
Logo for a lingerie boutique is a
flower and pubis. It is meant to be both
elegant and erotic.

103.2
Paul Woods
San Francisco, 1992
Woods + Woods
Logo for a grower of specialty
herbs and vegetables.

103.1

GOURMET
GARDENS

103.2

104

104.1

HEALTH

$\mathscr{P}$ AVILION

104.3

FIREFLY

RETAIL THEATRICS

104.2

TULIPE

RESTAURANT

104.4

104.1
Steve Curry/Jason Scheideman
Los Angeles, 1989
Curry Design
AD: Steve Curry
Logo for women's casual wear.

104.2
Kenichi Nishiwaki/Brian Jacobson
San Francisco, 1992
Profile Design
AD: Kenichi Nishiwaki
Logo for interior and environmental
designers.

104.3
Maureen Erbe
Logo for a healthcare clinic and health
education facility. It is meant to imply
health, growth and nurturing.

104.4
Harriet Briteboard
Los Angeles, 1989
Rod Dyer Group
AD: Rod Dyer
The casual logo is meant to imply that the
restaurant is as well.

105.1
James McKiernan
Long Beach, 1991
Logo for "Desert Round-Up."

105.2
Clement Mok
San Francisco, 1990
Clement Mok Designs
Logo for a Las Vegas hotel and casino.
The logo is meant to convey a fantasy.

105.3
Jose Serrano
San Diego, 1990
Mires Design
AD: Jose Serrano
Illus: Dan Thoner
Logo for Palm Springs spring break.

105.1

105

105.2

105.3

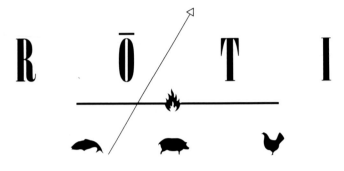

106.1

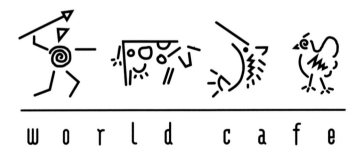

106.2

FOOD

106.1
Catherine Richards
Palo Alto, 1989
Arias Associates
AD: Mauricio Arias
Logo for a restaurant that specializes
in rotisserie entrees.

106.2
Susan Rogers
Santa Monica, 1991
Rusty Kay & Associates
AD: Rusty Kay
Logo for a restaurant with a
primitive, modern Mayan-
African theme.

107.1
William Reuter
San Francisco, 1990
William Reuter Design
AD: William Reuter
Illus: Lisa Ray
Logo for a group that plans
parties at restaurants.

107.2
William Reuter
San Francisco, 1989
William Reuter Design
Logo for a restaurant, the plate is
also a "C"

107.3
Constance Beck
Santa Monica, 1990
Beck & Graboski
AD: Terry Graboski
Logo for the Art Deco Hollywood
Roosevelt Hotel night club.

107.1

107.2

107.3

108.1

108.1
Margo Chase/Lorna Stovall
Los Angeles, 1988
Margo Chase Design
AD: Margo Chase
The logo is a flaming mustard jar! For a
division that specializes in salsa music.

109.1
Bill Murphy
Los Angeles, 1989
Rod Dyer Group
AD: Rod Dyer
The logo implies a classic, artistic,
enjoyable trattoria.

109.2
Lauren Smith
Palo Alto, 1991
Logo for a chain of upscale
wine shops.

109.3
Rick Tharp
Los Gatos, 1992
Tharp Did It
Logo for a publisher of books
on wine label design. The logo
indicates the position of a label on a
wine bottle.

109.4
Vince Rini
Los Angeles, 1992
Siegel & Gale/Cross
AD: Jim Cross
Logo for a wine auction, the mark
indicates the environment of Santa
Barbara -- sun, mountains, sea and
Spanish architecture.

TRATTORIA

109.1

109.3

SANTA BARBARA WINE AUCTION

109.2

109.4

110.1

110.3

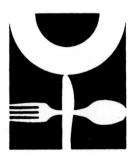

110.2

110.1
Greg Berman/Peter Sargent
Los Angeles, 1990
Sargent & Berman
Logo was created to sell this product
in Italy, as a California alternative to
classic Italian desserts.

110.2
Cheryl Savala
Newport Beach, 1992
The McAdams Group
AD: Larry McAdams
Logo for Women's Foodservice
Forum

110.3
Anthony Luk/Kenichi Nishiwaki
San Francisco, 1990
Profile Design
AD: Kenichi Nishiwaki
Logo for a custom candy
manufacturer.

111.1
Mark Fox
San Rafael, 1987
Black Dog
AD: Matthew Drace
Logo for annual food awards given
by San Francisco Focus Magazine.

111.2
Scott Mires
San Diego, 1991
Mires Design
AD: Scott Mires
Illus: Tracy Sabin
Logo for a travel incentive program
to Kona, Hawaii. The mark is an
attempt to capture the flavor of the
island.

111.3
Tony Hyun
Los Angeles, 1990
The Graphics Studio
AD: Gerry Rosentswieg
Logo for an upscale coffee shop.

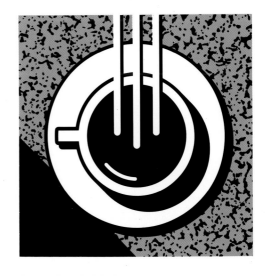

111.1

111

111.2

111.3

50TH ANNIVERSARY
OF THE WORLD'S FAIR
·TREASURE ISLAND·

112.1

ARCHITECTURE
112.1
Mark Fox
San Rafael, 1988
Black Dog
Logo based on themes from the 1939
World's Fair.

113.1
Heather Wielandt
Los Angeles, 1992
Siegel & Gale/Cross
AD: Jim Cross
Logo, for a real estate company, shows a
gated entrance to waterfront property.

113.2
Paula Sugarman/Brad Maur
San Diego, 1992
Page Design
AD: Paul Page
Logo for an architectural firm implies the
innovative design of small structures.

113.3
Wayne Hunt
Pasadena, 1988
Wayne Hunt Design
Logo for the Architectural Foundation of
Los Angeles refers to the LA City Hall
and classic architectural devices.

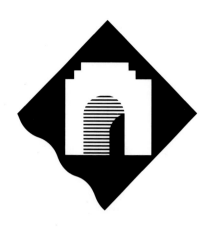

113.1

113.2

113.3

114.1

114.1
Gerald Reis
San Francisco. 1989
Gerald Reis & Company
Logo for a garden paraphernalia store;
the intent was to suggest, through a
variety of forms, a contemporary
reference to the 18th Century world
of the English garden.

115.1
Jennifer Morla/Jeanette Aramburu
San Francisco, 1990
Morla Design
AD: Jennifer Morla
Logo developed for architectural firms
who sponsor this contest for children.
It is intended to be playful and whimsical.

115.2
Mark Allen
Venice, 1989
Logo for a small publishing venture. Profits
go into buying the owners' first home.

115.3
Paul Woods
San Francisco, 1985
Landor Associates
AD: Dwight Woodfield
Logo for the San Francisco Fair.

FIRST HOUSE

PRESS

115.1

115.2

115.3

116.1

116.2

116.1
James Guerard
Marina del Rey, 1989
Robert Miles Runyan & Associates
AD: Robert Miles Runyan
Logo for a real estate developer.

116.2
Katherine Lam/Paula Yamasaki-Ison
Los Angeles, 1986
Patrick SooHoo Designers
AD: Patrick SooHoo
Logo for the museum gift shop takes its
design from the stair step
motif of the architecture.

117.1
Alan Disparte/Timothy Harris
San Francisco, 1990
Timothy Harris Design
AD: Timothy Harris
Urban Eyes is an ultra hip eyeglass store
in the middle of the city.

117.2
Dan McNulty
Los Angeles
Georgopolis Design
AD: John Georgopolis
Logo for a real estate promotion.

117.3
Margo Chase
Los Angeles, 1986
Margo Chase Design
The logo signifies the two cities, New York
and Los Angeles, where the company does
business.

117.4
Josh Freeman/Vickie Sawyer
Los Angeles, 1987
Josh Freeman/Associates
AD: Josh Freeman
Logo for a recreation and dining club
located in a group of three circular towers.

117.1

117.2

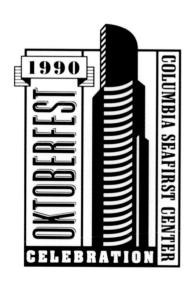

117.3

117.4

METRO

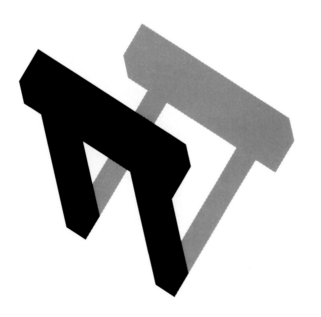

118

118.1
Jay Vigon
Los Angeles, 1989
Vigon Seireeni
The logo for a housing development
company suggesting an architectural "M"
bathed in sunlight.

118.2
Dennis DeBasco
Los Angeles, 1988
The Graphics Studio
AD: Gerry Rosentswieg
The proposed logo for Gateway West.
The image is an arch that has shadows
forming the letter "W".

119.1
Gary Baker
Santa Monica, 1988
Baker Design Associates
Logo for a classical music radio station,
the image is based on the classic capital,
an ear and a violin.

119.2
Peter Sargent/Wilson Ong
Los Angeles, 1985
Bright & Associates
AD: Keith Bright
Logo for a typographer uses the
basic shapes and forms of typography.

119.3
Anonymous Graphics
Santa Barbara, 1990
Logo for a university art museum.

119.4
Anonymous Graphics
Los Angeles, 1990
Logo for a shop that sells classic
Italian leather goods.

119.5
Julia Tam
San Francisco, 1990
Rabuck & Fox
Logo for a store that sells classic
women's clothes.

119.1

119.3

119.2

SCARPA

119.4

119.5

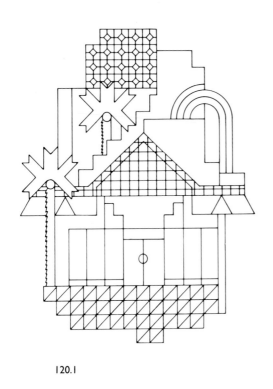

120.1

120.2

120.3

120.4

120.1 + 120.2
Gerry Rosentswieg
Los Angeles 1988
The Graphics Studio
Logo/icons for a series of shopping
malls. The images are abstractions of
the architecture.

120.3
Maureen Erbe
Los Angeles. 1989
Logo for electric pumps
for reservoirs.

120.4
John Coy
Los Angeles, 1991
Coy, Los Angeles
Logo for central business
and cultural district.

121.1
Jay Vigon
Los Angeles, 1990
Proposed logo for Il Tetto, a hat shop.
The name means the roof in Italian.

121.2
William Reuter
San Francisco, 1988
William Reuter Design
AD: William Reuter
Illus: Sukey Bryan
Logo for Live-in Care.

121.3
Sandra McHenry
San Francisco, 1990
Sandra McHenry Design
AD: Sandra McHenry
Illus: Ward Schumaker
Logo for a coalition of non-profit
housing developers. The mark shows
the generosity of giving a home to
the homeless.

121.1

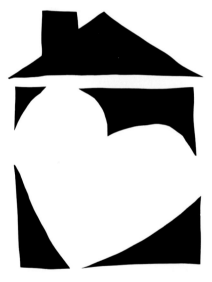

121.2

San Francisco Transitional Housing Fund

121.3

122.1

122.2

122.1
Clive Piercy
Los Angeles, 1988
Rod Dyer Group
AD: Rod Dyer
Logo for a restaurant/lounge that features jazz. The logo is an attempt to capture the rhythms and counter-point of the legendary musician Bix Beiderbeck.

122.2
Michael Schwab
Sausalito, 1991
Michael Schwab design
AD: Shari Shryock
Logo for a fashion event with music.

123.1
Bill Corridori
Venice, 1991
Bright & Associates
AD: Keith Bright
Logo for music schools. The image is meant to be simple and imply that learning can be easy.

123.2
Michael Patrick Cronan
San Francisco, 1990
Logo for a summer symphony series.

123.3
Larry Vigon/Brian Jackson
Los Angeles, 1992
Larry Vigon Studio
AD: Larry Vigon
Logo with the musical note on fire suggests that the music is hot.

123.4
Jodi Royer
Sacramento, 1991
Logo for the California Symphony.

123.1

EMBR
PRODUCTIONS
MUSIC

123.3

123.2

123.4

124.1

KOZ

124.2

124.3

124.1
Joe Miller
San Jose, 1991
Joe Miller's Company
Logo for a radio station, designed to imply that
the music is "lotsa fun, zow and listen up".

124.2
Mark Fox
San Rafael, 1990
Black Dog
AD: Tommy Steele/Jeff Fey
Logo for recording artist Dave Koz.

124.3
Glenn Sakamoto
Los Angeles, 1991
Stan Evenson Design
AD: Stan Evenson
Logo for a best of music series
for a recording company.

125.1
Christine Haberstock
Los Angeles, 1991
Logo for a jazz musician suggests that the
player is cool, relaxed, with sensuous lips,
all relating to the sound of the instrument.

125.2
Stan Evenson
Los Angeles, 1992
Stan Evenson Design
Logo for a recording company; the
image is a square peg in a round hole.

125.3
Stan Evenson
Los Angeles, 1991
Stan Evenson Design
Logo for classic album conversion to
CD for a recording company.

125.1

125.2

125.3

STREAM LINE GRAPHICS

126.1

126.2

126.3

OBJECTS

126.1
Stan Evenson
Los Angeles, 1989
Logo for a specialty stat house.

126.2
Brad Curtis
San Francisco, 1990
Logo for a retailer of fine reconditioned
vintage autos. The image is meant to
appeal to people who want to drive
something "classic, ferocious or fun."

126.3
Stan Evenson
Los Angeles, 1987
Stan Evenson Design
Logo for a stat house, the image
implies quick turn around.

127.1
Mark Fox
San Rafael, 1990
Black Dog
AD: Carole Layton
Ag: Pentagram
Logo for magazine article on latchkey
kids who cook for themselves.

127.2
Joe Miller
San Jose, 1988
Joe Miller's Company
Logo for events on public radio that
benefit the homeless. The simple
imagery, hand cut illustration and
words are basic and appeal for help.

127.3
Thomas McNulty/Brian Jacobson
San Francisco, 1991
Profile Design
AD: Thomas McNulty
The logo was designed for the person-
nel at Apple; they're intelligent, creative
and off-the-wall. The intent was to
create a logo that would seem friendly.

127.1

127.2

127.3

128

128.1

128.2

128.3

128.1
Michael Brock/Nancy Nimoy
Los Angeles, 1989
Michael Brock Design
AD: Michael Brock
Department logos created for LA Style
magazine. These "Matisse-ish" quick,
sometimes whimsical, marks are visual
representations of department subjects.

128.2
Raymond Wood/BillCorridori
Venice, 1991
Bright & Associates
AD: Keith Bright/Ray Wood
The logo for Speedway Cafe is a racing
tire and wing reminiscent of hood
ornaments of the 30's and 40's.

128.3
Maureen Erbe
Los Angeles,1991
Logo for the LA Metro, the mark is
intended to convey a casual, fun,
smart look, implying that riding this new
train will be a smart and efficient way to
travel Los Angeles.

129.1
Scott Brown
Palo Alto, 1989
Michael Patrick Partners
AD: Duane Maidens
Logo for Letter Perfect, the hand drawn
letter is meant to show a spontaneous
response to the client's postage needs.

129.2
Glenn Martinez
Santa Rosa, 1990
Glenn Martinez and Associates
Logo for a special event for the Red
Cross uses "simple, frivolous illustration
and goofy type" for its appeal.

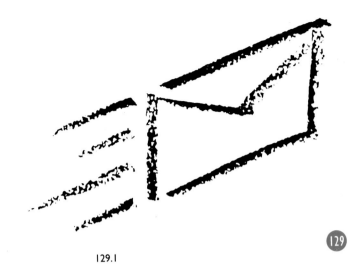

129

129.1

S H O E S
W I T H !
W I N G S

129.2

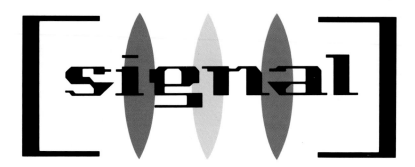

130.1

130.2

130.3

130.1
Margo Chase/Lorna Stovall
Los Angeles, 1990
Margo Chase Design
AD: Margo Chase
Proposed logo for a rock band, the mark is an abstraction of a traffic signal; it is intended to be masculine, urban and strong.

130.2
Joe Miller
San Jose, 1991
Joe Miller's Company
Logo for a business form manufacturer, the mark is a visual reminder of multi-part snap-out forms, as well as the connotation of organization, efficiency and computerized handling.

130.3
Mike Salisbury
Los Angeles, 1990
Mike Salisbury Communications
Logo for a clothing manufacturer who makes street style clothing with a punk attitude, clothes on the cutting edge.

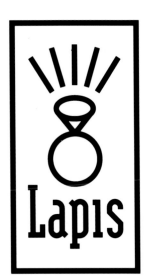

131.1

131.1
Maureen Erbe
Los Angeles, 1990
Icons created for the education programs
of the LA performing arts center. The
programs are history, visual arts, bus-in
programs, music, the Music Center
building, and dance.

131.2
Sarajo Frieden
Los Angeles, 1989
Personal logo showing the "well
worn tool."

131.3
Paul Curtin
San Francisco, 1991
Paul Curtin Design
Logo for Lapis Technologies.

131.2

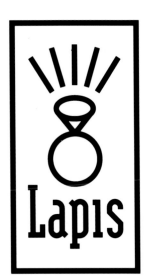

131.3

132.1

132.4

132.2

132.5

132.3

132.6

132.1-132.2
Clement Mok
San Francisco, 1987
Clement Mok Designs
Icons for Apple Computers.

132.3
Gerry Rosentswieg
Los Angeles, 1987
The Graphics Studio
Symbol developed for men's
room identification in
The Peters Group offices.

132.4
Christine Nasser
Malibu, 1991
Symbol for Food in Art,
an exhibition of paintings
and photographs.

132.5
Dana Shields
San Francisco, 1992
CKS Partners
Symbol for Chronicle Books

132.6
Gerry Rosentswieg
Los Angeles, 1987
The Graphics Studio
Symbol developed for
women's room for
The Peters Group offices

133.1
Stan Evenson
Los Angeles, 1992
Stan Evenson Design
Logo for a radio program.

133.2
Bob Dinetz
Los Angeles, 1990
Vrontikis Design Office
AD: Petrula Vrontikis
Logo for a group of storyboard artists.
The positive and negative shapes show
the uniqueness and interpretation that
each of the artists bring to a project.

133.3
Mike Salisbury
Los Angeles, 1991
Mike Salisbury Communications
Logo for McClatchy Films, utilizes the
initial "M" , a high-tech view finder and
film registration marks, to characterize
this film editing company.

133

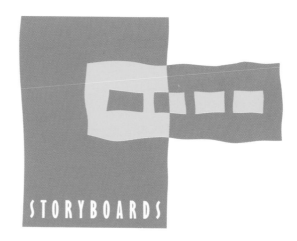

133.1

133.2

133.3

134.1
Donald Craig
Menlo Park, 1992
Fulcrum Design
Logo for brokers of printing and
packaging that shows the inter-
connection of the two.

134.2
Ross Carron
San Francisco, 1992
Ross Carron Design
Logo that shows an abstraction of a
tape reel and a diskette for a software
and computer consulting firm.

134.3
Mamoru Shimokochi
Los Angeles, 1991
Shimokochi Reeves Design
Studio promotional logo implying
motion and that the studio is "tops."

135.1 - 135.5
Jennifer Morla/Sharrie Brooks
San Francisco, 1992
Morla Design
AD: Jennifer Morla
Logo series for MTV Sports uses
symbols to communicate categories,
such as the screaming mouth for
"Thrill," the single hand for "Solo" and
the brain for "Endurance," etc. The
dotted arrows unify them.

inTEGRATED
P R O D U C T S

134.1

Datastructure

134.2

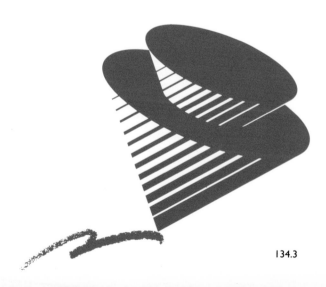

134.3

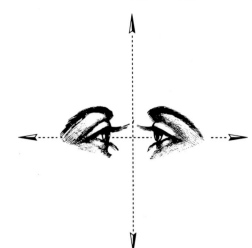

ENDURANCE

135.1

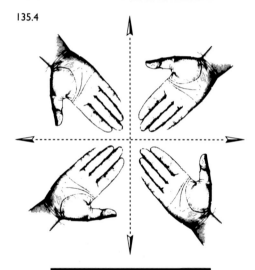

COMPETITION

135.4

135

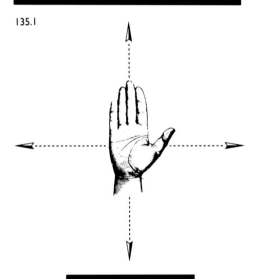

SOLO

135.2

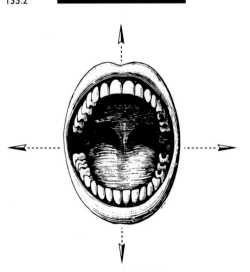

GROUP

135.5

THRILL

135.3

136.1

136.1
Craig Frazier
San Francisco, 1992
Frazier Design
Logo for a film production house.

136.2
Jay Vigon
Los Angeles, 1991
Logo for photographer Alan Shaffer.

136.3
Ruediger Goetz
San Francisco, 1992
Zimmermann Crowe Design
AD: Dennis Crowe
Logo for Eco Crusader, a promotional
logo for Levi's Sweats.

137.1
Michael Patrick Cronan
San Francisco, 1991
Cronan Design
Icon series created for The Walking
Man line of clothing.

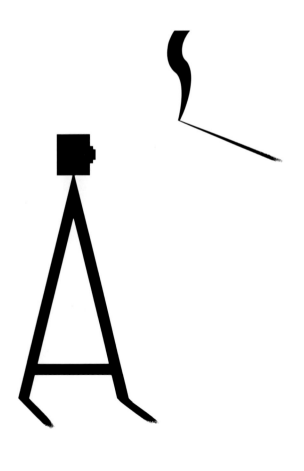

136.2

136.3

safety

music

welcome

neatness

broadcasting

utility

documentation

manufacturing

architecture

enthusiasm

collaboration

travel

comfort

nutrition

hospitality

artifacts

137.1

138.1

138.2

SHAPES
138.1
Jay Vigon
Los Angeles, 1990
Vigon Seireeni
Logo for a film production company
shows a man (the director) casting a
larger than life-sized image.

138.2
Sally Hartman Morrow
San Francisco, 1990
Coleman Souter
AD: Mark Coleman
Logo for Western Medical.

139.1
Cinne Worthington
San Francisco, 1989
Coleman Souter
AD: Michael Souter
Logo for a hair salon.

139.2
John White/Aram Youssefian
Long Beach, 1991
White Design
AD: John White
Studio logo is made up of positive and
negative, the basic tools of graphics.

139.3
Chris Garland
Los Angeles, 1992
Garland, CA
Logo for an electronic bulletin board,
the black button is symbolic of the
buttons that activate the system.

139.4
Clive Piercy
Santa Monica, 1989
Ph.D
AD: Clive Piercy/Michael Hodgson
Logo for a women's swimwear
manufacturer. "In a marketplace full of
garish, over-designed logos, raisins is
meant to stand out because of its under-
stated, non-design nature. It is meant to
generate curiosity and interest."

139.1

WHITE W DESIGN

139.2

139.3

R A I S I N S

139.4

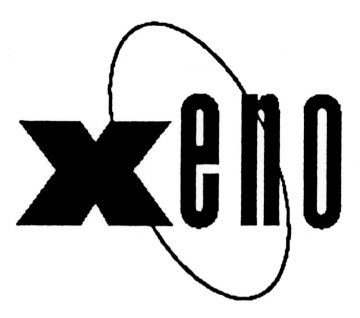

140.1

140.2

140.1
Chris Garland
Los Angeles,1991
Garland, CA
Studio logo built on the computer.

140.2
Zuzanna Licko
Berkeley, 1988
Logo for a computer generated
and oriented magazine.

141.1
Scott Brown
Palo Alto, 1991
Michael Patrick Partners
AD: Dan O'Brien/Duane Maidens
Logo for Dexxa, a computer mouse.
The arrows within the "X" are what the
users see when using the product, the
"D" is for product recognition.

141.2
Gary Robert Baker
Santa Monica, 1988
Baker Design Associates
Logo for an international container
transport service. The circle indicates
the globe, the horizontal bars indicate
speed and technology, as well as being
associated with train loading equipment.

141.3
Mike Salisbury/Cindy Luck
Los Angeles, 1988
Mike Salisbury Communications
Self-promotional logo.

141.4
Gerry Rosentswieg
Los Angeles, 1991
The Graphics Studio
Logo of an "L" shape and a tire.

141.5
Jay Vigon
Los Angeles, 1991
Studio identification logo.

141.6
Glenn Martinez
Santa Rosa, 1990
Logo for a television and theatrical
producer made up of a spotlight and
shadow.

141.1

141.2

141.3

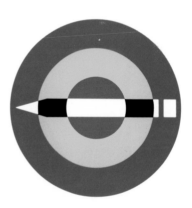

141.4

141.5

141.6

California Lottery

142.1

142.2

142.1
Mark Bergman
San Francisco, 1988
SBG Partners
AD: Nicolas Sidjakov
Logo, made up of the simplest shapes, is intended to be seductive and exciting.

142.2
Mike Salisbury/Mark Kawagami
Los Angeles, 1991
Mike Salisbury Communications
AD: Mike Salisbury
Proposed logo for a film, *Meteor Man*, made up of a planet shape and the letter "M".

143.1
Mamoru Shimokochi
Los Angeles, 1992
Shimokochi Reeves Design
Logo for a radio station.

143.2
James Falkner
Los Angeles, 1989
Rod Dyer Group
AD: Rod Dyer
Logo that implies a radio service as big as the universe.

143.3
Clive Piercy
Santa Monica, 1991
Ph.D
AD: Clive Piercy/Michael Hodgson
Logo for a women's swimwear manufacturer. The logo is meant to conjure up the feel of old radios and also have a surf/beach feeling. It is supposed to be hip, fun and ambiguous. (What is Radio Fiji?)

W A R P

143.1

SUPERAUDIO.

CABLE RADIO SERVICE™

143.2

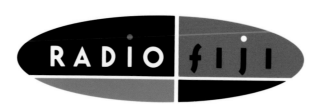

143.3

144.1

144.1
Jay Vigon
Los Angeles, 1989
Logo for a private school. The three
basic shapes of design looked at from
different perspectives illustrates the
schools progressive attitude.

145.1
Brian Collentine
San Francisco, 1986
AXO design studio
"X" marks the spot. This is a studio that
solves visual problems. "A" stable is
connected by the "X" to "O" unstable.
The mark is intended to imply solid, stable
and creative design solutions.

145.2
David Gilmour
San Francisco, 1991
Coleman Souter
AD: Mark Coleman
Logo for New Ways To Work, an
innovative work/temp agency.

145.3
Victoria Miller
Los Angeles, 1990
Victoria Miller Design
Logo for fast-food, Italian take-out, in the
clean Italian style. The wavy line is reminis-
cent of a lasagna noodle, the arrows
indicate "to go".

145.4
Gerald Reis
San Francisco, 1986
Gerald Reis & Company
The logo is derived from the Indian word
Deepa, or flame, and made appropriate for
a fabric designer of the same name.

145.1

145.3

145.2

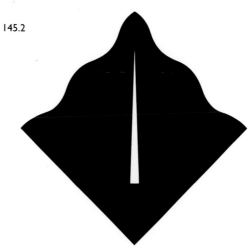

145.4

SIGNETS/SHIELDS
146.1
Paul Woods
San Francisco, 1991
Woods + Woods
Logo for luggage takes the form of a
passport style stamp.

147.1
Arne Ratermanis
San Diego, 1991
Ted Hansen Design Associates
AD: Ted Hansen
Logo for copywriter Carm Greco.

147.2
Dennis Crowe/Neal Zimmermann
San Francisco, 1990
Zimmermann Crowe Design
Logo to indicate that stretch doesn't have
to mean "old man pants."

147.3
Margo Chase
Los Angeles, 1989
Margo Chase Design
AD: Jeri Heiden
Logo for album cover; the mark uses reli-
gious icons to create a medallion/shield.

147.4
Michael Patrick Cronan/Linda Lawler
San Francisco, 1989
Cronan Design
AD: Michael Patrick Cronan
Logo for a film production company.

146.1

147.1

147.3

147.2

147.4

148.1

148.1
Margo Chase
Los Angeles, 1986
Margo Chase Design
Studio logo, the flames are
creativity and green for youth,
the shield contains an icon that
is an abstracted "MCD". It is
intended to appear enigmatic,
eclectic and unusual.

149.1
Kathy Warinner
Larkspur, 1991
Aufuldish & Warinner
Logo for a photographer, the circle
of dots suggest a camera lens, the
monogram suggests a face or aperture.
The simplicity and symmetry imply a
steadfast devotion to craft and quality.

149.2
Margo Chase
Los Angeles, 1989
Margo Chase Design
Personal Mark.

149.3
Margo Chase
Los Angeles, 1989
Margo Chase Design
Logo for a rock band, based on
heraldic devices and incorporating
the double "B" monogram and
the alchemical eye for power.

149.4
Romane Cameron
Los Angeles, 1992
Studio Seireeni
AD: Richard Seireeni
Logo for a sophisticated, elite
line of men's wear.

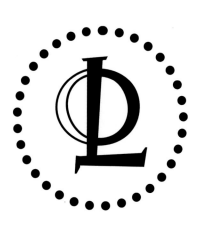

149.1

149.3

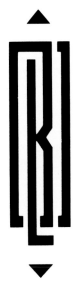

149.2

149.4

150.1

150.2

150.1
AlbertTreskin/Gerald Reis
San Francisco, 1992
Gerald Reis & Company
Logo that uses traditional island
forms and imagery.

150.2
Margo Chase
Los Angeles, 1990
Margo Chase Design
Logo for a recording company.

151.1
Margo Chase
Los Angeles, 1990
Margo Chase Design
Personal signet.

151.2
Margo Chase
Los Angeles, 1989
Margo Chase Design
Logo for a guitar company.

151.3
Lorna Stovall
Los Angeles, 1991
Lorna Stovall Design
Personal mark for a wedding invitation.
"T" for the bride, "M" for the groom.

151.4
Margo Chase
Los Angeles, 1991
Margo Chase design
Logogram for Virgin Records.

151.5
Margo Chase
Los Angeles, 1990
Margo Chase Design
Initial mark/seal for fine
artists' organization.

151.1

151.3

151.4

151.2

151.5

INITIALS

152.1
Clive Piercy/Michael Hodgson
Santa Monica, 1988
Ph.D

152.2
Richard Patterson
Los Angeles, 1990
Sargent & Berman
AD: Peter Sargent/Greg Berman

152.3
Raymond Wood
Los Angeles, 1990
Bright & Associates
AD: Keith Bright
Logo for a printer.

153.1
Gerald Reis
San Francisco, 1989
Gerald Reis & Company
Logo for a textile designer,
Beverly Thome.

153.2
Clive Piercy/Michael Hodgson
Santa Monica, 1990
Ph.D
Logo for Bima Entertainment Group.

153.4
Richard Patterson
Los Angeles, 1989
Sargent & Berman
AD: Peter Sargent/Greg Berman
Logo for Decorate-It! an innovative
room decorating system for children.
The mark emphasizes the versatile
and playful nature of the product.

153.5
Jim Pezzullo
Los Angeles, 1989
Studio Seireeni
AD: Richard Seireeni

152

152.1

152.2

152.3

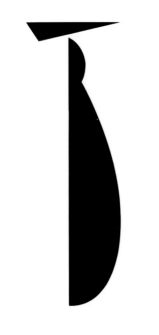

153.1

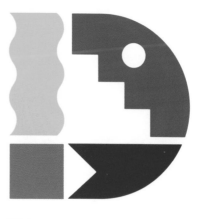

153.4

153.2

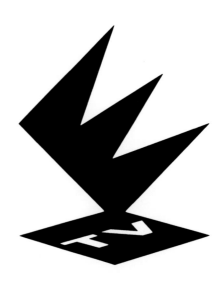

**ENTERTAINMENT
TELEVISION**

153.5

153.3

GAIN

154.1

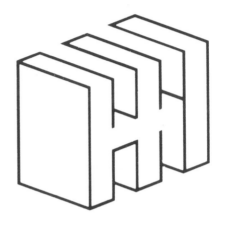

154.3

154.2

154.4

154

154.1
Jack Herr
San Francisco, 1991
Clement Mok Designs
AD: Clement Mok

154.2
Margo Chase
Los Angeles, 1992
Margo Chase Design
Logo for Geffen Records.

154.3
Michael Hodgson
Los Angeles, 1984
Logo for Hennessey + Ingalls, Art and
Architecture Books.

154.4
Bob Aufuldish
Larkspur, 1991
Aufuldish & Warinner
Big "H" is the nickname for a woman who
does a variety of things. The mark is odd
enough to appeal to her audience and
simple enough to do different kinds of
work under one name/logo.

155.1
Mamoru Shimokochi
Los Angeles, 1990
Shimokochi Reeves Design
AD: Anne Reeves
Logo for the shops at the
Hong Kong Airport.

155.1

156.1

JAYRO

156.2

156.3

156.1
Scott Brown
Palo Alto, 1991
Michael Patrick Partners
AD: Michael Patrick
Logo for Inter-City
Transit System.

156.2
Romane Cameron
Los Angeles, 1991
Studio Seireeni
AD: Richard Seireeni
Logo for a clothing
designer/manufacturer.

156.3
Rick Jackson
Irvine, 1990
Rick Jackson & Associates
Personal mark for designer.

157.1
David Rose
Mountain View, 1990
Abrams Design Group
AD: Colleen Abrams

157.2
Raymond Wood
Venice, 1988
Bright & Associates
AD: Keith Bright
Logo for LA Sports, a council to bring
international sporting events to LA.

157.3
Maureen Erbe
Los Angeles, 1989
Logo for Left Bank, a restaurant.

157.4
Don Weller
Los Angeles, 1984
The Weller Institute for the
Cure of Design.
Logo for a printing firm. Lithographix.

LASER WORKS

157.1

157.3

157.2

157.4

158.1

158.2

MILANO
AT EASTLAKE GREENS

158.4

158.3

158.5

158.1
Mike SalisburyMark Kawagami
Los Angeles, 1991
Mike Salisbury Communications
AD: Mike Salisbury
Proposed logo for the movie
Meteor Man

158.2
Mike Salisbury/Terry Lamb
Los Angeles, 1991
Mike Salisbury Communications
AD: Mike Salisbury
Logo for "Game Play" Mattel Games.

158.3
Mike Salisbury/Terry Lamb
Los Angeles, 1991
Mike Salisbury Communications
AD: Mike Salisbury
Logo for Mattel Games.

158.4
Catherine Sachs
San Diego, 1991
Mires Design
AD: Scott Mires
Illus: Miguel Perez
Logo for a housing development
using an eclectic mix of new and
old architectural styles to convey a
sense of the new California lifestyle.

159.4
Robert Overby
Los Angeles, 1986
Logo for a children's book, titled
Eye Nose Eye Smile.

159.1
Jay Vigon
Los Angeles, 1992
Logo for a clothing manufacturer.

159.2
Maureen Erbe
Los Angeles, 1988
Logo for a fast food restaurant.

159.3
Glenn Martinez
Santa Rosa, 1988
Personal mark for the studio.

MASTERPIECES

159.1

CALIFORNIA MELT

159.2

159.3

160.1

160.3

160.2

160.4

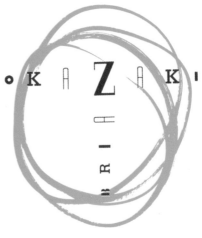

160.5

160.1
Vicki Adjani
Santa Monica, 1989
Baker Design Associates
AD: Gary Baker
Logo for the Nestor Group.

160.2
Ken Hegstrom/Kecki Williams
Auburn, 1990
Hegstrom Design
AD: Ken Hegstrom
Logo for a graphic design trade school.

160.3
Romane Cameron
Los Angeles, 1991
Studio Seireeni
AD: Richard Seireeni
Logo for a restaurant.

160.4
Ellen Roebuck
Los Angeles, 1988
Logo for an artists' rep,
Onyx Enterprises.

160.5
Margo Chase
Los Angeles, 1992
Margo Chase Design
Personal mark for
Brian Okazaki.

161.1
Dan McNulty
Los Angeles, 1990
Georgopoulos Design
AD: John Georgopoulos
Logo for Pacific Business Interiors,
an interior design firm.

161.2
Dan McNulty
Los Angeles, 1992
McNulty & Co.
Logo for a company that
manufactures bicycle hubs.

161.1

161.2

162.1

162.1
Kevin Mason
Santa Monica, 1990
Logo for architectural contractors,
Ramco, a firm that specializes in
housing restorations.

163.1
Michael Manwaring/Paul Chock
San Francisco, 1987
The Office of Michael Manwaring
AD: Michael Manwaring
Logo for Robinson, Mills and
Williams, Architects.

163.2
Liz Hecker
Sausalito, 1988
Liz Hecker Design
Logo for RMF, owner and operator
of amusement/entertainment type
businesses.

163.3
Sean Alletorre/Tom Bouman
Los Angeles, 1989
Coy, Los Angeles
AD: John Coy
Logo for the Riordan Foundation.

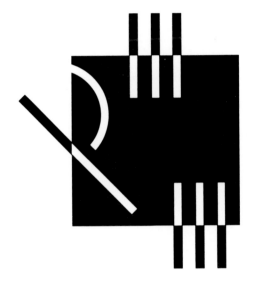

163.1

163.3

163.2

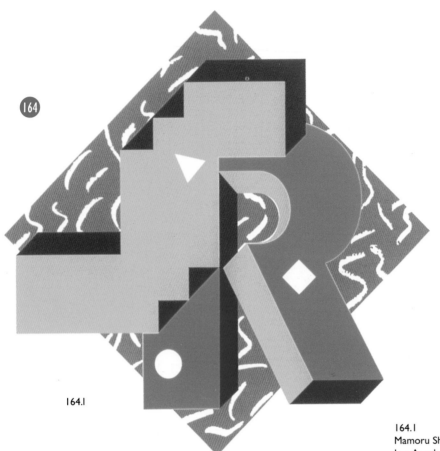

164.1

164.1
Mamoru Shimokochi
Los Angeles, 1991
Shimokochi Reeves Design
AD: Anne Reeves
Promotional logo for studio.

165.1
Lorna Stovall
Los Angeles, 1990
Lorna Stovall Design
Logo for S.S. Enterprises.

165..2
Steve Curry
Los Angeles, 1987
Curry Design
Logo for Skilset Typographers.

165.3
Jay Vigon
Los Angeles, 1992
Logo for a film production company.

165.2

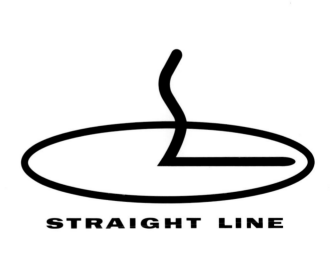

165.1

165.3

165

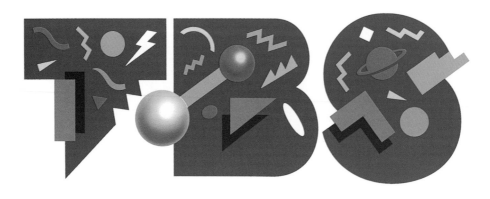

166.1

166.2

U C L A

SCHOOL OF THEATER
FILM AND TELEVISION

166.3

166.1
Mamoru Shimokochi
Los Angeles, 1990
Shimokochi Reeves Design
Logo for Tokyo Broadcasting System.

166.2
William Reuter
San Francisco, 1989
William Reuter Design
Logo for Top Copy, a desktop
publishing service bureau.

166.3
Mamoru Shimokochi
Los Angeles, 1992
Shimokochi Reeves Design
AD: Anne Reeves

167.1
Michael Manwaring
San Francisco, 1985
The Office of Michael Manwaring
Logo for Eileen West, a women's
clothing manufacturer.

167.2
Jay Vigon
Los Angeles, 1988
Vigon Seireeni
Logo for a men's
sportswear company.

167.3
Gregory Thomas
Los Angeles, 1988
Logo for Barry Zauss Associates,
an architectural rendering company.

167.1

ZYLOS

167.2

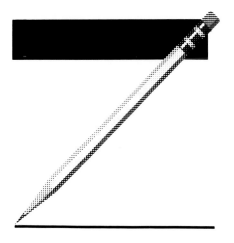

167.3

168.1

169.1

169.2

NUMBERS
168.1
John Coy
Los Angeles, 1987
Coy Los Angeles
25th anniversary logo for
UCLA College of Fine Arts.

169.1
Mark Palmer/Pat Kellogg
Palm Desert, 1991
Mark Palmer Design

169.2
Larry Vigon/Brian Jackson
Los Angeles, 1991
Larry Vigon Studio
AD: Larry Vigon

170.1

170.1
Michael Patrick Cronan
San Francisco, 1990
Cronan Design
Logo for Ten Squared Structural
System, a display and storage system.

170.2
John Coy
Los Angeles, 1989
Coy, Los Angeles
Anniversary logo.

170.3
Andy Engel
Los Angeles, 1990
Capitol Records
AD: Tommy Steele

171.1- 171.4
Michael Patrick Cronan
San Francisco, 1989
Cronan Design
Series of logos for
Studio Eight Software.

170.2

170.3

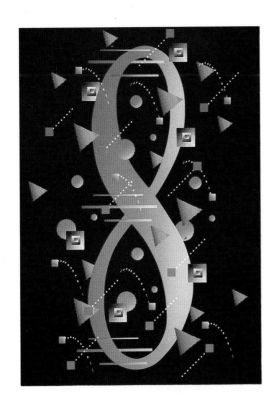

171.1

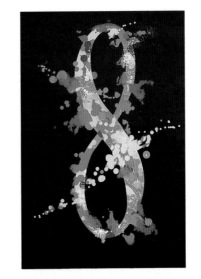

171.2

171.3

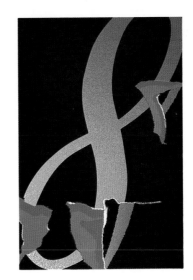

171.4

APPLE'S TENTH ANNIVERSARY

172.1

172.1
Clement Mok
San Francisco, 1986
Clement Mok Designs
AD: Clement Mok
Illus: Hugh Dubberly

173.1
Denis Parkhurst
Los Angeles, 1986
Ken Parkhurst & Associates
AD: Ken Parkhurst
Logo for the 16/32 Microprocessor.

173.2
Elizabeth Henry
Playa Del Rey, 1987
Robert Miles Runyan
AD: Robert Miles Runyan
40th anniversary logo for
the LA Rams.

173.3
Mark Galarneau
Palo Alto, 1986
Galarneau + Sinn

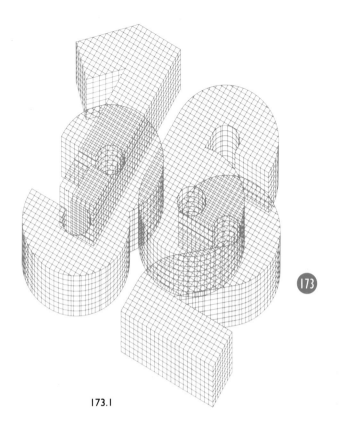

173.1

173.2

Octagon

173.3

173

174.1

174.2

TYPE

174.1
Richard Atkins
Los Angeles , 1988
Coy, Los Angeles
Logo for the Los Angeles
Music Center Opera.

174.2
Clive Piercy/Michael Hodgson
Santa Monica, 1992
Ph.D
Logo for an ergonomic office chair.

175.1
Clement Mok/Chuck Routhier
San Francisco,, 1989
Clement Mok Designs
AD: Clement Mok
Logo for software.

175.2
Yee-Ping Cho
Los Angeles, 1992
Baker Design Associates
AD: Gary Baker
Logo for a software company.

175.3
Tom Devine
Burbank, 1989
Devine Design
Logo for a R&R Band.

175.4
Clement Mok/Chuck Routhier
San Francisco, 1988
Clement Mok Designs
AD: Clement Mok
Logo for an optical, character
recognition, software package.

TENpointO

175.1

logik*e*

175.2

LaZyTOWN

175.3

omniPAGE™

175.4

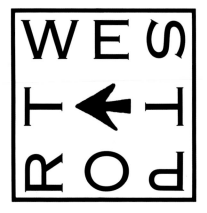

176.1

176.3

176.2

176.4

176.1
Gerald Reis
San Francisco, 1988
Gerald Reis & Company
Logo for a line of chairs.

176.2
Ken Parkhurst
Los Angeles, 1990
Ken Parkhurst & Associates
Logo for a business tower.

176.3
Bruce Yelaska
San Francisco, 1987
Bruce Yelaska Design
Logo for a restaurant.

176.4
Maureen Erbe
Los Angeles, 1987
Maureen Erbe Design

177.1
Petrula Vrontikis
Los Angeles, 1988
Vrontikis Design Office
Logo for a copywriter,
Eileen Antonier.

177.1

piIIar

178.1

178.2

LIMITED EDITION WEARABLES BY CONTEMPORARY ARTISTS

AUBERGINE BARBARA

179.1

179.3

YOU AROUND All's

179.2

HOME EXPRESS

179.4

180.1

180.1
Michael Manwaring
San Francisco, 1986
The Office of Michael Manwaring
Logo for a winery.

181.1
Joe Miller
San Jose, 1991
Joe Miller's Company
Logo for a new music magazine.

181.2
Paul Curtin
San Francisco, 1992
Curtin Design
Logo for developers of semiconductor
surface mount packaging.

181.3
Paul Woods
San Francisco, 1988
Woods + Woods
Logo for Electronics for Imaging,
software that produces color output.

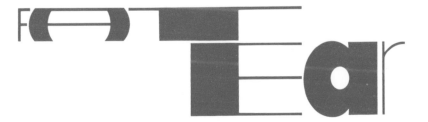

181.1

SMART

181.2

181.3

182.1

182.2

182.1
Mike Salisbury/Dave Parmley
Los Angeles, 1992
Mike Salisbury Communications
AD: Mike Salisbury
Logo for a line of boy's clothing.

182.2
Dan Riley
San Mateo, 1992

183.1
Thomas McNulty
San Francisco, 1991
Profile Design
Logo for an in-house restaurant at
Apple Computer, based on the clock
and time.

183.2
Bruce Yelaska
San Francisco, 1991
Bruce Yelaska Design
Logo for an employee
incentive program.

183.1

183.2

184.1

184.3

184.2

184.1
John Bielenberg/Kathy Warinner
San Francisco, 1989
Bielenberg Design
AD: John Bielenberg
Logo for modular toothbrush.

184.2
Clive Piercy/Michael Hodgson
Santa Monica, 1990
Ph.D
Logo for a product design firm.

184.3
Tracy Titus
San Diego, 1987
Page Design
AD: Paul Page
Illus: Sherrill Cortez
Logo for a mobile hair salon.

184.4
Clive Piercy
Santa Monica, 1991
Ph.D
AD: Clive Piercy/Michael Hodgson
Logo for a photographer

185.1
Mark Allen
Venice, 1991
Mark Allen Design Associates
Logo for a software company.

BRET LOPEZ

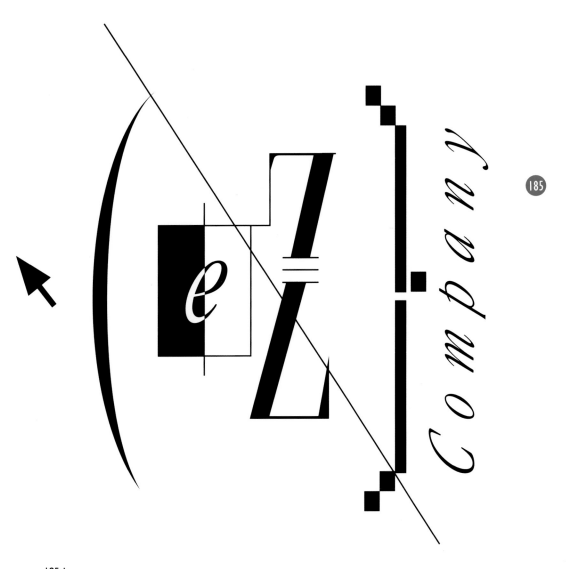

185.1

186.1

186.2

186.3

186.1
Pamela Racs
Los Angeles, 1992
Mark Taper Forum Graphics
Logo intended to communicate
a non-traditional performance
of a classic play.

186.2
Stan Evenson
Los Angeles, 1990
Stan Evenson Design
Logo for a typesetter.

186.3
Jim De Luise
Santa Monica, 1990
De Luise Design

187.1
Victoria Miller
Los Angeles, 1989
Victoria Miller Design
Logo for a line of
tennis sportswear.

187.2
Larry Vigon/Brian Jackson
Los Angeles 1991
Larry Vigon Studio
AD: Larry Vigon
Logo for stylists.

187.1

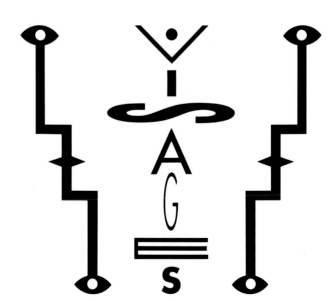

187.2

188.1

SAN'WICHES

188.2

SOMBA

188.3

188.4

188

188.1
Jay Vigon
Los Angeles, 1987
Vigon Seireeni
AD: Jay Vigon Richard Seireeni
Logo for a restaurant.

188.2
Gabrielle Mayeur
Venice, 1989
Bright & Associates
AD: Keith Bright
Logo for a restaurant.

188.3
Paul Woods
San Francisco, 1991
Woods + Woods
Logo for South of Market
Business Association.

188.4
Rick Tharp
Los Gatos, 1990
Tharp Did It
Logo for a winery.

189.1
Margo Chase
Los Angeles, 1992
Margo Chase Design
Logo for a tee shirt design.

189.2
Sarajo Frieden
Los Angeles, 1989
Logo for a book store.

189.1

189.2

PROPA GANDA

190.1

190.2

ITAMI FILMS INC.

190.3

190.1
Mark Fox
San Rafael, 1988
Black Dog
Logo and typeface design.

190.2
Mark Sackett
San Francisco, 1992
Sackett Design
Illus: Wayne Sakamoto
Logo for LAX magazine.

190.3
John Clark
Los Angeles, 1991
Siegel & Gale/Cross
AD: Jim Cross
Logo for a film production company.

191.1
Lorna Stovall
Los Angeles, 1992
Vrontikis Design Office
AD: Petrula Vrontikis
Logo for a restaurant.

191.2
Mike Salisbury/Tim Clark
Los Angeles, 1985
Mike Salisbury Communications
AD: Mike Salisbury
Proposed logo for a motion picture.

191.3
Margo Chase
Los Angeles, 1987
Margo Chase Design
Personal logo for Kathy Guild.

191.1

191.2

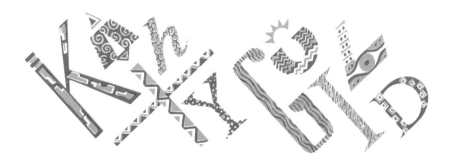

191.3

192.1

192.2

192.3

192.1
Margo Chase
Los Angeles, 1987
Margo Chase Design
Logo for a rock band.

192.2
Margo Chase
Los Angeles, 1990
Margo Chase Design
Logo for a fashion show.

192.3
Sally Hartman Morrow
San Francisco, 1989
Coleman Souter
AD: Mark Souter
Logo for a paper company's
award program.

193.1
Mamoru Shimokochi
Los Angeles, 1991
Shimokochi Reeves Design
AD: Anne Reeves

193.2
Margo Chase
Los Angeles, 1992
Margo Chase Design
Logo for Starfax Video Co.

193.3
Zuzanna Licko
Berkeley, 1989
Emigre Graphics
Logo for a typeface.

193.1

193.2

193.3

194.1

194.1
Richard Patterson
Los Angeles, 1992
Sargent & Berman
AD: Peter Sargent
Logo based on a compass design.

194.2
Gerry Rosentswieg
Los Angeles, 1992
The Graphics Studio
AD: Gerry Rosentswieg
Illus: Mark Carrel
Logo for printer's self-promotion.

195.1
Kathy Warinner
San Francisco, 1991
Bielenberg Design
AD: John Bielenberg
Logo for shoe made
from recycled materials.

195.2
Alan Disparte
San Francisco, 1992
Alan Disparte Design
Personal logo for a movie
set designer/art director.

195.3
Bruce Yelaska
San Francisco, 1990
Bruce Yelaska Design
Logo for a restaurant.

195.4
Stan Evenson
Los Angeles, 1990
Stan Evenson Design
Promotional logo for
recording artists.

194.2

D E J A

195.1

195.3

195.2

195.4

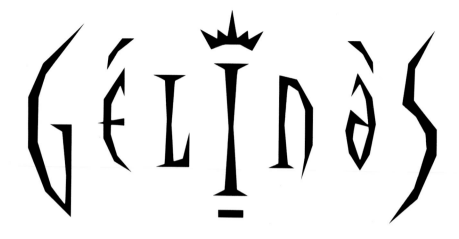

196.1

196.2

196.3

196.1
Margo Chase/Lorna Stovall
Los Angeles, 1989
Margo Chase Design
AD: Margo Chase
Logo for a line of beauty products.

196.2
Margo Chase/Lorna Stovall
Los Angeles, 1988
Margo Chase Design
AD: Margo Chase
Logo for Esprit T-shirt line.

196.3
Margo Chase
Los Angeles, 1992
Margo Chase Design
Logo for a film.

197.1
Margo Chase
Los Angeles, 1991
Margo Chase Design
Self-promotional logo.

197.2
Margo Chase
Los Angeles, 1991
Margo Chase Design
Logo for a rock band.

197.1

197.2

197

198.1

198.2

198.3

198.1
Margo Chase
Los Angeles, 1986
Margo Chase Design
Proposed logo for a movie title.

198.2
Margo Chase/Lorna Stovall
Los Angeles, 1989
Margo Chase Design
AD: Margo Chase
Logo for a restaurant.

198.3
Jennifer Morla
San Francisco, 1992
Morla Design
Logo for a restaurant.

199.1
Mark Allen
Venice, 1991
Mark Allen Design Associates
Logo for a recording artist.

199.2
John Pappas
San Francisco, 1990
Zimmermann Crowe Design
AD: Neal Zimmermann/Dennis Crowe
Logo for an artists' rep.

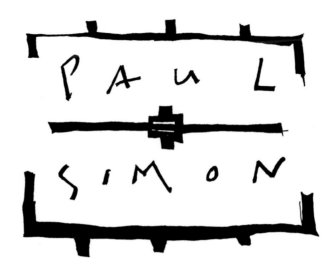

199.1

199.2

200.1

200.2

200.1
Margo Chase
Los Angeles, 1988
Margo Chase Design
AD: Tommy Steele
Logo for recording company
at a new music seminar.

200.2
Linda Warren/Kimberly Hillman
Venice, 1992
Warren Group
Logo for athletic equipment
and clothing manufacturer.

201.1
Lorna Stovall
Los Angeles, 1991
Lorna Stovall Design
Logo for a Capitol Records
in-house publication.

201.2 + 201.3
Margo Chase
Los Angeles, 1992
Margo Chase Design
Self-promotional logos.

201.4
John Coy
Los Angeles, 1991
Coy, Los Angeles
Event logo.

CAPITOL

201.1

201.3

201.4

201.2

ART DIRECTORS & ILLUSTRATORS

SPECIAL THANKS

I would like to thank my production assistant Lisa
Woodard for her patience and unfailing good humor
whenever I changed my mind and my layouts.
Also I want to thank Anita Bennett who prods me into
writing and then cleans up my mess.